MATH GRADE 4

WARM-UPS

Developing Fluency In Math

$$2.7 < 2\frac{9}{10}$$

C =
A =

Written by **Sheri Disbrow**
Illustrated by **Stephanie O'Shaughnessy**

Prufrock Press Inc.
P.O. Box 8813
Waco, TX 76714-8813
Phone: (800) 998-2208
Fax: (800) 240-0333
http://www.prufrock.com

Introduction

Do You Need Another Math Book?

If you already use a basal text, do you really need another math book? For most teachers, the answer is "yes." This supplementary math book reinforces the concepts presented in basal texts, giving additional, consistent review of the most important math concepts that are presented at this grade level. Even teachers who use a basal text will find it necessary to give additional practice to assure that students have a concrete grasp of mathematical concepts. **Math Warm-Ups** is challenging and spirals in content and difficulty, making it the perfect math supplement.

Math Warm-Ups and Math Standards

This is one in a series of supplementary math text books. Each book is a daily math workbook, designed to meet math standards for a specific grade level. This book was developed according to the national, Ohio, and Texas content standards and objectives for fourth grade.

Each page of **Math Warm-Ups** offers ten problems that deal with a variety of concepts. The problems address the following math standards:

- understand the meaning of addition and subtraction
- ability to compute fluently and make estimates
- recognize and extend patterns
- name and draw two- and three-dimensional shapes
- apply transformation
- measure using various units or systems
- represent data in pictures and graphs
- analyze data
- apply appropriate strategies to solve problems
- use the language of mathematics to express mathematical ideas.

What's So Great About This Book?

This book consistently exposes students to a variety of concepts in all objective areas including common sense. It is quick and easy for the teacher to grade and provides immediate and repeated opportunities for re-teaching. **Math Warm-Ups** is designed to aid the teacher in covering all objectives and provide students with opportunities to practice all of the math objectives within a five day period. It stimulates learning and encourages the use of different problem solving techniques. The advantages of using this text are that it:

- is easy to grade
- motivates students
- provides daily diagnosis of students' weaknesses
- covers a variety of objectives
- spirals in level of difficulty
- consistently builds critical thinking and problem solving skills
- addresses problem solving daily in small pieces
- combines multiple objectives into several questions
- presents multi-step problems
- asks open-ended questions
- supports the existing curriculum
- eliminates "holes" in learning, thus enabling students to meet standards
- can be used individually or with a whole class
- provides a quick diagnosis of new students' abilities
- addresses all objectives on a regular basis
- enables productive parent conferences, pinpointing problem areas
- assists teachers in finding weak areas where instructional focus is needed.

How to Use the Book

This workbook is designed to be used in a variety of ways. It can be used as a warm-up, as homework, or as a diagnostic tool. You can use it as a daily or weekly review or as additional practice to supplement your regular math instruction.

Teachers, parents, and administrators can use this book to diagnose weak areas and assure the conceptual understanding of the students on a daily basis. Parents, students, and teachers can evaluate progress which will allow them to identify and correct deficiencies. It empowers students and motivates them to invest in their own learning. Parents who want to make sure that their children have mastered math skills and will be ready for any testing situation will find this workbook thorough and easy to use. Additionally, teachers who want to provide individual practice for students who are ready to move faster through the curriculum than the rest of the class can use these exercises and be comfortable that students are getting practice in a broad spectrum of math skills.

The **Math Warm-Ups** series came out of a need to ensure students' success while developing mathematical thinkers and problem solvers. It has been tested and used in the classroom with great success. Students who use these exercises are interested and motivated because they are given repeated opportunities to be successful. Practicing annual expectations and goals on a daily basis, builds student self-esteem and confidence, while improving attitudes and grades. Enjoy the book and the rewards that come with it.

Exercise 1

Use the figure to answer 1, 2, and 3.

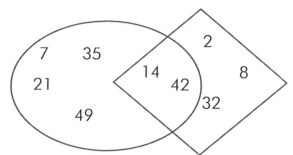

1. The numbers in the diamond are multiples of what number?

   _____

2. The numbers in the oval are multiples of what number?

   _____

3. The numbers in both the oval and the diamond are common multiples of both _____ and ____.

....

4. What is the time difference between these two clocks?

   _____ hours and _____ minutes

....

5. Insert <, =, or > to make this a true number sentence.

   1,263 ⬭ 1,213

6. 120,157
    − 21,859
    _____

....

7. 1,768   5)1,265
    ×   5
    _____

....

8. Round to the nearest thousand.

   35,129 _____

   2,741 _____

....

9. (216+12) − 123= _____

....

10. Banners in the gym must be hung from longest to shortest. The tennis banner is 76 inches long, the baseball banner is 54 inches long, the football banner is 84 inches long, and the volleyball banner is 66 inches long.
    In what order should they be hung?

Exercise 2

1. Connect these triangles with their names.

   scalene   a.

   equilateral   b.

   isosceles   c.

2. Complete the fact family.

   5×7 = ____ $35 \div 7$ = ____

   ____ × ____ = ____

   ____ ÷ ____ = ____

3. Complete the pattern.

   $\dfrac{1}{5}$, $\dfrac{3}{5}$, $\dfrac{5}{5}$, ____, ____

   The rule is _____

4. James had $10.00. He bought 2 erasers that cost 55¢ each and a notebook that cost $5.00. How much change did he get?

   $ _____

5. 2 weeks = ____ days

   3 weeks = ____ days

   2 weeks + 3 days = ____ days

6. Write a decimal for:

   eighty-eight and seventy-three hundredths

   _____

7.
8,156	3,456
− 4,361	+ 789

8. What is the value of **3** in 12,537?

   _____

9. What is the area and perimeter of this object?

   5 cm.

   7 cm.

   A = _____

   P = _____

10. For the highway cleanup project three schools collected the following amounts of trash.

    Sunnnyside   4,642 kg.
    Teach   5,001 kg.
    Brightway   3,967 kg.

    How many more kilograms did Teach collect than Sunnyside? _____

    How many kilograms of trash were collected by all three schools?

    _____

Exercise 3

Name _____

1. Fill in the missing fractions.

```
├──┼──┼──┼──┼──┼──┼──┼──┼──┤
1        1½        2   2¼          3
```

2. This is a regular octagon.

How many congruent triangles could you draw to completely fill the octagon?

_____

3. Julie has half of a dozen butterflies. Alexa has 3/4 of a dozen butterflies. How many butterflies does each girl have? Who has more?

Julie - _____   Alexa - _____

_____ has more butterflies.

4. Complete the fact family.

$6 \times 4 =$ ____

$24 \div 6 =$ ____

____ $\times$ ____ $=$ ____

____ $\div$ ____ $=$ ____

How does knowing these facts help you solve 6×40 and $240 \div 6$?

_____

_____

5.
```
  100        32        132
×   5       ×5        ×  5
```

6.
```
  80
  ×6          6)540
```

7. Round the prices to even ten cents.

 = $1.23   = $1.79   = 32¢

_____   _____   _____

What could you buy with $4.00?

_____

8. Which number has a 2 in the hundreds place?

   a. 127.43   **b.** 249.17   **c.** 742.99

9.
```
 189,000          189,101
- 25,000         - 24,976
```

10. Jack has $6.29 and Laura has $10.21. How much more money does Laura have than Jack?

   $ _____

Exercise 4

1. Drew has half a dollar, Marcy has 35¢, and Damien has a quarter. Write each amount as a decimal, in order of least to greatest.

_____   _____   _____

2. Which shapes are hexagons? _____

Which shapes are symmetrical? _____

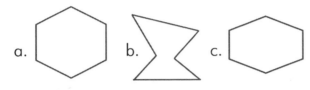

a.   b.   c.

3. Write a fraction for the part of leaves that are white. Reduce it to its simplest form.

4. Jane's family drove to Florida. They started at 6:00 a.m. and drove until 5:00 p.m. How many hours did they drive?

_____ hours

5. Cara has $3.70. She wants to buy some candy that costs 50¢, 75¢ and $1.00 for each piece. List three possible combinations of candy that she could buy.

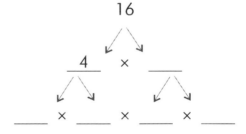

_____

_____

_____

6. Insert <, =, or > to make this a true number sentence.

8.21 ⬭ 5.73

7.
$$45{,}001 + 3{,}589$$
$$605{,}102 - 125{,}573$$

8.
$$54.39 - 33.30$$
$$69.54$$
$$2.51$$
$$+ .43$$

9.
$$800 \times 5 \qquad 24 \times 5 \qquad 824 \times 5$$

10. Complete this factor tree.

16

4 × _____

_____ × _____ × _____ × _____

Exercise 5

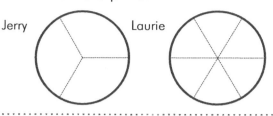

Name _____

Use the departure times for the three buses to answer questions 1, 2, and 3.

Bus A	1:10 p.m.	2:20 p.m.	3:30 p.m.	4:40 p.m.
Bus B	9:30 a.m.	10:30 a.m.	12:30 p.m.	1:30 p.m.
Bus C	8:00 p.m.	9:00 p.m.	10:00 p.m.	

1. How long are the intervals between departure times for bus A?

_____

2. How long are the intervals between departure times for bus C?

_____

3. Which bus would you have to take if you get off of work at 7:30 p.m.? _____

How long would you have to wait?

_____

4. Write the names of these polygons.

_____   _____

5. Insert <, =, or > to make these true number sentences.

8 × 8 ◯ 6 × 7

2 × 3 ◯ 10 × 0

2 × 9 ◯ 18 × 1

6. Laurie has 2/6 of a pizza. Jerry has 2/3 of a pizza. Shade to show who has more pizza.

Jerry   Laurie

7.
```
  642        642
 ×10        × 12
____        ____
```

8.
```
 $92.85      $10.50
+  7.21      −  7.49
_____      _____
```

9. Put these numbers in order from **smallest to largest**.

1.99   2.01   1.89   2.10

_____ _____ _____ _____

10. Write the numbers that are 1,000 more than each of these numbers.

2,003 _____

506 _____

13,491 _____

157,034 _____

87 _____

Exercise 6

1. Mary Beth divided 56 marbles into 4 equal groups. How many marbles are in each group?

   _____ marbles in each group

2. What is the value of **5** in the number 75,101.34?

   _____

3. Alex is 166 cm tall. Taylor is 1.65 m tall. Who is taller? _____

   How much taller is he? _____

4. Draw lines and shade the circle to show 2/8.

5. Draw a rectangle on this grid that has an area of 24 square units.

6.
9,000	12,101
−7,389	−1,980

7. (10 x 2) + 1 = _____

   (5 x 4) + 8 = _____

8. Estimate your answer first and then solve.

   problem   estimate

   658

   × 20

9. Draw hands on the clock to show 6 hours and 20 minutes after 2:00 p.m.

   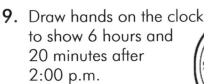

10. The soccer team took in $4,892.67 for the fund raiser during the month of May. In June they took in $1,999.98. Estimate the total amount of money that they took in for both months.

    They collected about $_____.

Exercise 7

Name _____

1. 1 meter = 100 centimeters

   1½ meters = _____ centimeters

   2 meters = _____ centimeters

   2 ½ meters = _____ centimeters

2. Complete the pattern.

   3, 10, 17, 24, ____, ____, ____

   The rule is _____

3. (2+6) + 4 = 2 +(6 + ___)

4.
   $$1,999 - 295$$

   $$34$$
   $$78$$
   $$+ 51$$

5. Fill in the missing points on the number line.

   5.0   5.1   5.4

6. There are 144 cards in Robert's baseball card collection. How many pages does he need, if he can put 8 cards on each page?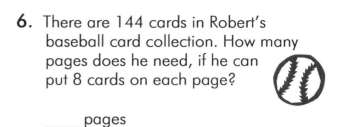

   ____ pages

7. Draw a regular pentagon. Draw a line of symmetry.

8. Write 4,312 in expanded form.

   _____

   _____

9. $5{\overline{)246}}$

   $$7495 \times 23$$

10. Thomas lives to the left of James. Brad lives in the house that has a number divisible by 8. James's address is 100 less than Jill's address. Match each person with their address.

    Jill   Brad   Thomas   James

    | 12 | 22 | 122 | 160 |

Name _____

1. The attendance at the mall on Thursday was 20,193 people. On Friday 27,193 people went to the mall.

   What is the estimate of how many people were at the mall on both Thursday and Friday?

   _____ people

2. Beth has 3/10 of the candy bar. Carrie has 2/5 of the same size candy bar. Shade these two candy bars. Who has more candy?

   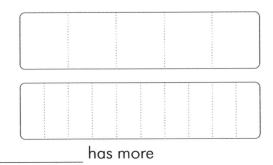

   _____ has more

3.
62	62	62
×9	×10	×11

4. If this scale is balanced, what is the weight of A?

   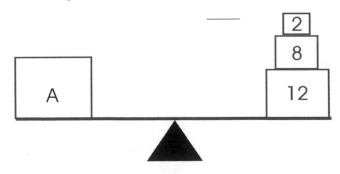

5. Write the decimal that shows how much is shaded. _____

   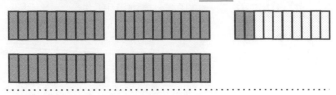

6. Write the number for:

   twenty-six hundredths

   _____

7. How much more liquid is in container A than in container B? _____ ml.

   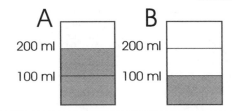

8. The auditorium at school holds 500 people. There are 25 rows. How many people can sit in each row?

   _____ people in each row

9. List the set of **odd** numbers between 60 and 70.

   _____

10.
608,396	45,703
− 25,199	+5,214

Exercise 9

1. Andrea's family is driving to Arizona. They average 55 miles per hour. The trip will take them 4 hours. How many miles will they travel?

   _____ miles

2.
   $$\begin{array}{r} 1.4 \\ +7.6 \\ \hline \end{array}$$
   $$\begin{array}{r} 76.9 \\ -34.5 \\ \hline \end{array}$$
   $$\begin{array}{r} \$5.98 \\ -1.25 \\ \hline \end{array}$$

3.
   $$\begin{array}{r} 7{,}601 \\ \times \quad 9 \\ \hline \end{array}$$
   $2\overline{)114}$

4. How can you divide these four pizzas evenly among three people? How much will each person get?

   _____ pizzas each

5. Hannah has $15.00. Dallas has 3 times as much money as Hannah. Rico has half of the amount of money that Dallas has. How much money does Rico have?

   Rico has $_____.

6. Twenty children had their pictures taken.
   - Half of the children bought 3 pictures.
   - A quarter of the children did not buy any pictures.
   - The other fourth of the children bought either 1 or 2 pictures.

   Show all of the combinations of pictures the children could have bought.

number of pictures			
3	2	1	0

7. Write the numeral for:

   five hundred thirteen thousand, four hundred fifty-five

   _____

8.
   $$\begin{array}{r} 900 \\ \times 60 \\ \hline \end{array}$$
   $$\begin{array}{r} 893 \\ \times 64 \\ \hline \end{array}$$

9. What are four letters in the alphabet that have vertical lines of symmetry?

   _____

10. If four people can get their hair cut in one hour, how long does it take for a haircut?

    _____ minutes

Exercise 10

1. Write the set of **even** numbers between eighty and ninety.

   _____

2.
900	900	912
×10	× 5	×15

   How do the first two problems help you estimate the answer to the third problem?

   _____

   _____

3. 70 x 6 = 210 + _____

4. (4+7) + 9 = 4 + (___ + 9)

5. Complete the fact family.

   9 x 4 = ___

   36 ÷ 9 = ___

   ___ x ___ = ___

   ___ ÷ ___ = ___

   Use these facts to quickly solve these problems.

   90 × 4 = _____

   9 × 40 = _____

   90 × 40 = _____

6. Draw arrays to show:
   (2 × 7) + (3 × 7) = 5 + 7

7. Hamburgers cost $3.45, onion rings are $1.50 and a drink is $1.75. If you have $10.00, do you have enough to also buy an ice cream for $1.25?

   _____

8. Write the numeral for:

   one and fourteen hundredths

   _____

9. Arrange these plants by height from **shortest to tallest**:

sunflowers	3.6 m.
gardenias	.45 m.
palm trees	6.2 m.
cacti	1.23 m.

10. Draw 2 parallel lines with a diagonal line that intersects both parallel lines.

Exercise 11

1. Laurie has a rectangular garden that is 5 feet wide and 7 feet long. Matt has a square garden that is 6 feet on each side. Who has more area in their garden? Draw a picture to illustrate your answer.

2. 1,726   552
   −957   × 4

3. Estimate and then solve.
   359
   47
   +866

4. Three times a number is 18. Write a number sentence to show how to find the missing number.

   _____

5. 1,000 grams = 1 kilograms

   2,000 grams = _____ kilograms

   2,500 grams = _____ kilograms

   6,000 grams = _____ kilograms

6. Write five tenths as a decimal and as a fraction.

   _____   _____

7. 896   896   896
   × 70   × 6   × 76

Use this diagram for questions 8, 9 and 10.

8. Name two streets that are parallel.

   _____   _____

9. If Central St. keeps going north, what street would it eventually intersect?

   _____

10. What street intersects at a right angle with Michigan Ave?

   _____

Exercise 12

1. The city of Tiffin had an election for mayor. The results were:

   Candidate A   324,681
   Candidate B   326,454
   Candidate C   300,589

   Round the totals to the nearest ten thousand and make a bar graph.

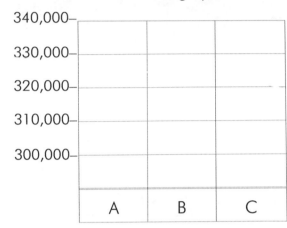

2. Write the four odd numbers after 642,000.

   _____   _____

   _____   _____

3. Round these numbers to the nearest hundred.

   80 _____   30 _____

   180 _____   290 _____

   1,180 _____   1,220 _____

4. 68
   × 7
   _____

   9)‾410

5. Complete the pattern.

   27, 24, 21, 18, ____, ____, ____

6. $12.57 $ 3.45 $.55
   – 9.58   +10.06   1.05
   _____   _____   +.69
                               _____

7. Write a 6-digit number that has a 3 in the hundreds place.

   _____

8. Order these numbers from **least to greatest**.

   14.29   4.263   41.99   8.642

   ____   ____   ____   ____

9. Insert <, =, or > to make this a true statement.

   $\dfrac{1}{12}$ ⬭ $\dfrac{1}{10}$

10. Aunt Julia's front porch is 6.1 meters in length and 5 meters in width. What is the area of the porch?

Exercise 13

1. Mary has received four grades on tests in English. They are 92, 93, 95, and 96.

   What is her average? _____

2. Complete the analogy.

   235 : 47 :: 175 : ____

   a. 35   b. 45   c. 40

3. $(3+6) + 4 = 3 + (6 + $ ____ $)$

4. The school turns off the air conditioning in the gym for 6 hours every day. How many minutes is this?

   _____ minutes

   If it costs $30.00 per hour to run the air conditioning, how much should the school charge to rent the gym for 2 hours?

   $ _____

5. $45.05
   − 40.95
   _____

   $ 2.60
   53.48
   + 6.37
   _____

6. Write the numeral for:
   24 and 72 hundredths

   _____

7. Write these decimals from **least to greatest**.

   6.901   36.25   645.8   2.892

   _____ _____ _____ _____

8. 800   900   894
   ×58   ×58   ×58
   ____   ____   ____

9. Make a bar graph to show these daily temperatures.

   Monday   75°
   Tuesday   80°
   Wednesday   68°
   Thursday   72°
   Friday   75°

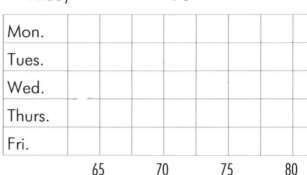

Mon.						
Tues.						
Wed.						
Thurs.						
Fri.						

              65   70   75   80

10. It is 8:30 a.m. and Emily is at an amusement park. She is going home in seven and a half hours. Show the time on the clock when she will be leaving.

    ____:____ p.m.

Exercise 14

1. Jack earned an 82 on his pretest test on Wednesday and an 89 on the final spelling test on Friday. If the teacher rounds his grades to the nearest 10, what will his grades be?

   pretest _____   final _____

2. Find the sum and difference.

   $\dfrac{4}{7} + \dfrac{1}{7} =$ $\dfrac{12}{15} - \dfrac{6}{15} =$

3. $6 \times (4+3) = (6 \times \underline{\quad}) + (6 \times \underline{\quad})$

   $= \underline{\quad}$

4.
   $\begin{array}{r} 800{,}467 \\ -543{,}957 \\ \hline \end{array}$ $\begin{array}{r} 100{,}539 \\ +349{,}259 \\ \hline \end{array}$

5. Drew is driving to a baseball game that is 180 miles away. He leaves at 9:00 a.m. and averages 60 miles per hour. Draw the hands on the clock below to show what time will he get there.

6. Draw a diagonal for each of these polygons.

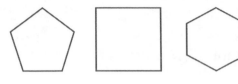

7. Complete the pattern.

   198, 197, 195, 192, _____, _____

   The rule is _____

8. Estimate the product before solving.

   estimate   problem

                          29
                         ×16
                         ____

9. Label the points 8.8, 9.3, and 9.6 on the number line.

   ├─┼─┼─┼─┼─┼─┼─┼─┼─┼─┼─┼─┤
   8.5   9.0   10.0

10. Write a decimal that tells how much is shaded.

    _____

Exercise 15

1. At the race track, the cars must line up in order from the smallest engine to the largest engine. The engine sizes are 2.4 liter, 1.9 liter, 2.04 liter, and 2.14 liter. In what order will the cars line up? Write the engine sizes from smallest to largest.

   _____ _____ _____ _____

2. Draw a symmetrical hexagon. Draw as many lines of symmetry as you can.

3. Michael practiced basketball for 240 minutes each day. How many hours did he practice?

   _____ hours

4.
400	471	500
× 5	× 5	× 5

5.
3,601	805,630
+4,009	−356,975

6. Round these numbers to the nearest thousand.

   980 _____   1,980 _____   3,920 _____

SEPTEMBER

SUN	MON	TUES	WED	THU	FRI	SAT
		1	2	3	4	5
6	7	8	9	10	11	12
13	14	15	16	17	18	19
20	21	22	23	24	25	26
27	28	29	30			

7. Yesterday was the 3rd of September. What is the date tomorrow? _____

8. The music teacher comes on even numbered Tuesdays and Thursdays. What dates will the music teacher come?

   _____

9. What will the date be four weeks after September 3rd?

   _____

10. Write fractions to show the part of the circles that are black.

    ○ ○ ○ ○ ●   ○ ○ ● ● ●
    ○ ○ ○ ○ ●   ○ ○ ● ● ●
    ○ ○ ○ ○ ●   ○ ○ ● ● ●
    ○ ○ ○ ○ ●   ○ ○ ● ● ●
    ○ ○ ○ ○ ●

    _____   _____

Exercise 16

Name _____

1. You have 36 feet of fence. Using whole numbers, draw three of the possible rectangles or squares you can make. Label the length and width.

6. 1 hour = _____ minutes

   2 hours = _____ minutes

   2 ½ hours = _____ minutes

   5 hours = _____ minutes

7. Insert <, =, or > to make this a true number sentence.

$$\frac{7}{12} \bigcirc \frac{3}{6}$$

8. Maggie cut a piece of rope **two and thirty two hundredths** meters long. How is this number written?

   _____

2. Calculate the area of each rectangle and square that you made.

   _____   _____

   _____

3. Which figure makes most sense for a toddler's play yard? Why? _____

   _____

4. Which fence area might be best for a dog run? Why ? _____

   _____

9. I am an even number less than 4,000 and greater than 3,000.
   I have 3 odd digits that are the same.
   What are all the possible numbers that I could be?

   _____   _____

   _____   _____

   _____

5. Complete the pattern.

   178, 169, 160, _____, _____, _____

   The rule is _____

10. Write a decimal for the shaded part.

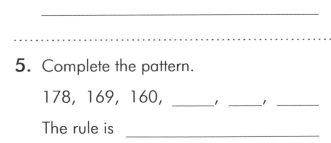

_____

© Prufrock Press Inc. • Math Warm-Ups Grade 4

Exercise 17

1. Write the numeral for:
nineteen thousand, six hundred forty-three

_____

2. This is how many stamps the post office sold in the first three months of the year:

January	20,056
February	19,850
March	25,859

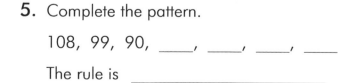

If the average stamp sold in the post office is 40¢, estimate how much money the post office received for the stamps.

January _____

February _____

March _____

3.

800,080	802,753
+600,002	−654,965

4. Write equivalent fractions.

$\frac{1}{2} = \frac{}{8}$ $\frac{1}{3} = \frac{}{12}$

5. Complete the pattern.

108, 99, 90, ____, ____, ____, ____

The rule is _____

6. Estimate the sum for:

$ 645.15
+ 463.29

7. Make a set of four 3-digit odd numbers that are related in some way.
Example: 122, 144, 166, 188

_____ _____ _____ _____

8. Trey has a can of marbles containing these marbles.

○ ○ ○ ○ ○ ● ● ● ◎ ◎ ◎ ◎ ◎ ◎ ◎ ◎

What is the probability that he will pick each type if he draws out one marble randomly?

P (○) = _____   P (●) = _____

P (◎) = _____

9. Find the sum.

$\frac{2}{7} + \frac{3}{7} = $ ____ $\frac{1}{12} + \frac{8}{12} = $ ____

10. Write names for these solid figures and tell how many faces each has.

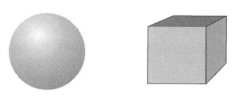

_____   _____

faces = _____   faces = _____

Exercise 18

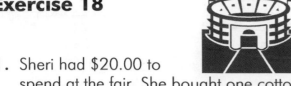

Name _____

1. Sheri had $20.00 to spend at the fair. She bought one cotton candy for $1.50. She bought two candy apples at $2.00 each. How much money does she have left?

   $_____

2. Write a fraction for the shaded part of each drawing.

 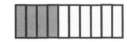

   _____   _____   _____

3. Complete the fact families.

   6 x 7 = 42   54 ÷ 9 = 6

   _____   _____

   _____   _____

   _____   _____

4. (3 + 8) + 2 = 3 + (8 + ___)

5. Jerry has 3/4 of a 16-inch pizza and Randy has 4/5 of a 16-inch pizza. Who has more pizza? _____

   Draw a picture to support your answer.

6. 9)180   525   525
                   × 5   ×10

7. Complete the table.

4	18	32	46	60	74	88
11	25					

8. Shawn has a baseball game in 1 hour and 25 minutes. It is 3:00 p.m. now. Show what time he needs to leave for the game if it takes 30 minutes to drive there.

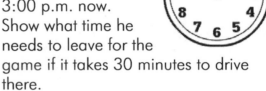

9. Estimate your answer to the second problem by doing the first problem.

   estimate   problem

   8)240   8)233

10. Write the numeral for:
    (1 x 1,000) + (5 x 100) + (4 x 10) + 8

    _____

Exercise 19

1. Round these numbers to the nearest thousand.

   13,400 _____

   17,890 _____

   156,300 _____

   ....

2. Label each of these geometric solids.

   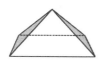

   _____   _____

   ....

3. If this is 1/9 of the total number of frogs in the pond, how many frogs are there?

   _____ frogs in all

   ....

4. Order these numbers from **greatest to least**.

   3,151   4,296   4,926   2,968

   _____ _____ _____ _____

   ....

5. Thursday there were 3,151 people at the mall. Each day there were 100 people more than the day before. How many people were at the mall on Wednesday and how many will be there on Sunday?

   _____ people on Wednesday

   _____ people on Sunday

6. Divide this spinner into eights. Using the letters A, B, C, and D make a spinner that would have the greatest probability of landing on A.

   ....

7. 7)385   7)409   7)3,850

   ....

8.
   ```
     5,000        7,602
   - 3,097      - 5,409
   ```

   ....

9. Shade to show 1/3 and write an equivalent fraction.

   $$\frac{1}{3} = \frac{}{12}$$

   ....

10. John is taller than Raul and Rex. Raul is taller than Bill and shorter than Rex. Show the order they they will be in if the line up from shortest to tallest.

Exercise 20

1. Fill in the numbers for points A, B, and C on the number line.

2. Three times a number is 210. Write an expression that could be used to find the number.

   _____

3.
```
  286              3,000
   14             − 365
+ 977             _____
_____
```

4.
```
471              471
×   3            ×   6
_____            _____
```

5. Casey made pancakes for herself and 7 friends. She made 40 pancakes. If all the girls ate the same number of pancakes how many did each girl eat?

   _____ pancakes each

   Write a fraction for the portion that each girl ate.

   _____

6. Insert <, =, or > to make this a true statement.

   345.6 ⬭ 345 ⁷⁄₁₀

7. Libby has 3/5 of a candy bar. Buzz has 7/10 of a candy bar. Shade the candy bars. Who has more?

   Libby | | | | |

   Buzz | | | | | | | | | |

8. Suzanne had $4.65 and then got $5.50 for allowance. Tracy has $8.80. Who has the most money? How much more?

   _____ has $ _____ more.

9. Caitlin has a dance class in 15 minutes. It lasts for 1 hour and 45 minutes. If it is 2:00 p.m. now, when will she be done? Show the time on the clock.

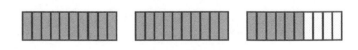

10. Write a decimal that represents the shaded portion.

   _____

Exercise 21

1. Write the number that is one less than **two million, sixty-seven thousand, three hundred thirty-eight**.

_____

2. On the first day of Kal's newspaper route he delivered 69 newspapers. Each day after that he got 3 new customers. If this pattern continues, how many customers will he have at the end of the fifth day?

day	1	2	3	4	5
newspapers	69				

3. How many newspapers did Kal deliver on the 4th day of his route?

_____ newspapers

4. If Kal makes 25¢ for each paper he delivers, how much did he make on the second day?

$ _____

5.

$167.54
+   1.95
_____

7,000
−6,432
_____

6. If c = 7, solve these number sentences.

c + 8 = ____

c + 59 = _____

8 × c = ____

7. The Smith family traveled 268 miles on the first day of their trip and 317 miles on the second day. How many miles did they travel in both days?

_____ miles

If they drove an average of 50 miles an hour, about how long were they driving?

_____ hours

8.

900
× 60

874
× 63

4)862

9. If this line is half of a longer line, how long is the longer line?

_____

_____ inches

10. If this is 1/4 of the valentines Russ received, how many did he receive in total?

____ valentines in all

Name _____

1. These are the profits in one month for two companies.

printing company	$58,139
paper company	$6,318,211

Estimate by rounding to the thousands how much more the paper company made than the printing company.

$_____

2. Tracy went to a double matinee that lasted 3 hours and 14 minutes. How many minutes did the movies last?

_____ minutes

3. Rebecca went to sleep at 9:30 p.m. She slept for 9 hours and 45 minutes. What time did she wake up?

____:____ a.m.

4.
857
× 8

6)1800

5. Insert <, =, or > to make these true statements.

7 x 6 ⬭ 8 x 5

4 x 6 ⬭ 2 x 12

3 x 9 ⬭ 4 x 8

Wild Animal Census

armadillo	🦔	🦔	🦔	🦔	
racoon	🦝	🦝	🦝	🦝	🦝
rabbit	🐇	🐇	🐇	🐇	🐇
fox	🦊	🦊	🦊		

each picture = 5 animals counted

6. How many more racoons were counted than:

armadillos _____   foxes_____

7. Altogether how many animals were counted?

_____ animals

8. This census represents animals counted in a 1 square mile area. If the ratios stayed the same, how many of each animal would you expect to find in a 6 square mile area?

armadillo_____   rabbit _____

racoon _____   fox _____

9. The students painted 3 stars in the first row, 7 stars in the second row, 11 stars in the third row and 15 stars in the fourth row. If they continue this pattern, how many stars will they paint in the next two rows?

____ and ____

10. (9 − 5) × 7 = (___ × 7) − (___ × 7)

Exercise 23

1. The Audubon Club counted all the birds they saw in one day. They saw 124 ducks, 13 egrets, and 17 geese. What was the total number of birds they observed?

   ____ birds

   How many more ducks did they count than geese?

   ____ more ducks

   If the club gets 2 points for each bird they count, how many points will they get for this one day?

   ____ points

2. I am a 3-digit **odd** number less than 400. All my digits are the same. What numbers could I be?

   _____   _____

3. Complete the pattern.

   3, 11, 17, 25, 31, ____, ____

   The rule is _____

4. Round to the nearest tenth.

   9.68   1.498   386.24

   _____   _____   _____

5. 805,073   894
   −436,846   ×70

6. Which of the lettered sections of this rectangle are congruent?

   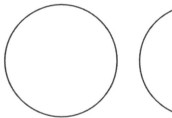

   ____ and ____   ____ and ____

7. Jane practiced piano for 180 minutes. How many hours was this? ____

   If she started at 3:00 p.m., what time did she finish?

   ____:____ p.m.

8. Draw lines and shade the circles to show 2/5 and 2/4. Circle the larger fraction.

9. Ten times a number is 90. Write an expression that could be used to find the number.

   _____

10. $(7 + 3) + 5 = 7 + ($ ___ $+ 5)$

Exercise 24

1. Jamie divided 320 sandwiches into 8 equal piles. How many sandwiches were in each pile?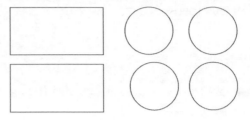

   _____ in each pile

2. Draw a right triangle, a parallelogram and a rhombus. Label each with the correct name.

3.
   2,000   340,560
   −599   +122,431

4. Complete the pattern.

   6⅛, 10⅜, 14⅜, _____, _____, _____

   The rule is _____

5. Round these numbers to the nearest hundred.

   2,756   12,816   165

   _____   _____   _____

6. (2+9) + 5 = ___ × ___

7. Cara has two bills and four coins in her pocket. The total value of the money is $6.20. The coins are all the same. What bills and coins does she have?

   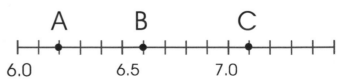

8. The temperature on Monday was 45°. The temperature increased by 19° on Tuesday. Shade the thermometer to show Tuesday's temperature.

9. Put these fractions in order from smallest to greatest.

   $\dfrac{6}{10}$ $\dfrac{3}{10}$ $\dfrac{1}{5}$ $\dfrac{4}{5}$

   ____   ____   ____   ____

10. What decimals would you write for points A, B, and C?

    A   B   C

    6.0   6.5   7.0

Exercise 25

Name _____

1. Nancy jumped rope for 300 seconds the first day, 600 seconds the second day and 900 seconds the third day. If this pattern continued how many seconds would she jump on the **fifth** day?

   _____ seconds

2. How many minutes did Nancy jump on the first day?

   _____ minutes

   How many minutes did she jump on the second day?

   _____ minutes

3. Write the numeral for:
   four hundred nineteen thousand, four hundred ninety-two and five tenths.

   _____

4. Rebecca bought a bracelet for $10.97, a necklace for $15.97 and earrings for $9.97. Estimate the total amount she spent.

   $_____

5. Write the decimals for points A, B, and C on the number line.

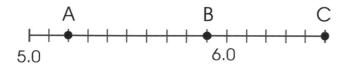

6. Find the area and perimeter of this rectangle.

   A = _____
   P = _____

   A different rectangle that would have the same area is a rectangle with:
   length = _____   width = _____

7.
$$2,561 \times 8 \qquad 369 \times 54 \qquad 9\overline{)786}$$

8.
$$\begin{array}{r} 900 \\ -500 \\ \hline \end{array} \qquad \begin{array}{r} 903.045 \\ -458.052 \\ \hline \end{array}$$

9. Write these factions as decimals.

   $\dfrac{2}{10}$ = _____ $\dfrac{6}{10}$ = _____

10. If $Z = T + 7$, find the value of Z for:

    T = 4   Z = _____

    T = 28   Z = _____

    T = 154   Z = _____

    T = 850   Z = _____

    T = 4,233   Z = _____

Exercise 26

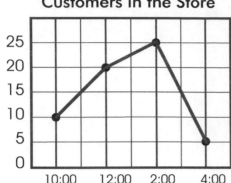

Customers in the Store

25
20
15
10
5
0

10:00   12:00   2:00   4:00

1. How many customers were in the store at these times?

10:00 a.m. _____

noon _____

2:00 p.m. _____

4:00 p.m. _____

2. What was the average number of customers in the store during the day?

_____ people

3. These are the times for three swimmers in the swim meet. Round each time to the closest second.

Jason   88.53 sec.   _____

Cody   88.12 sec.   _____

Jillian   87.55 sec.   _____

4. Jack has 16 buckets with 7 pounds of pecans in each bucket. How many pounds of pecans does he have in all?

_____ pounds

5. $ 19.70 $347.89
       +16.92   − 78.22

6.   200   198   8)942
        ×70   × 76

7.   400,000   400,842
       −300,000   − 284,715

8. Insert < or > to show the relative value of the fractions.

$\frac{9}{10}$ ◯ $\frac{9}{15}$

$\frac{3}{10}$ ◯ $\frac{3}{5}$

9. A + 16 = 40

A = ____

10. Carrie brought a dress for $29.00 and a pair of shoes for $36.92. Mary brought a pair of shoes for $67.92. Who spent the most and how much more?

_____ spent $ _____ more.

Exercise 27

Name _____

October

Sun	Mon	Tues	Wed	Thurs	Fri	Sat
				1	2	3
4	5	6	7	8	9	10
11	12	13	14	15	16	17
18	19	20	21	22	23	24
25	26	27	28	29	30	31

1. Mrs. Chin wears her Hawaiian dresses on even-numbered days. She reads Hawaiian folk tales on Mondays and Fridays. How many days will she wear her Hawaiian dress and read folk tales?

   _____ days

2. Becky washes dishes on odd-numbered days. She gets 25¢ each time she washes dishes. How much will she earn this month?

   $_____

3. 4)8600   4)8593

4. If Y ÷ 3 = 20, which problem would you use to find the value of Y?

   a. 20 ÷ 3   **b.** 20 × 3   **c.** 20 + 20

5. Raul had $6.25 and James had three times as much. How much money did James have?

   $ _____

6.
$$\begin{array}{r} 1.978 \\ +18.7 \\ \hline \end{array} \qquad \begin{array}{r} 23.205 \\ -14.2 \\ \hline \end{array}$$

7. The children lined up for a picture the following way:
   • 5 children on the bottom step
   • 9 children on the second step
   • 13 children on the third step
   Continuing this pattern, how many children were on the fifth step?

   _____ children

8. Insert <, =, or > to make these statements true.

   900 grams $\bigcirc$ 1 kilogram

   1,000 milligrams $\bigcirc$ 1 gram

   2,500 milligrams $\bigcirc$ 2 grams

9. Write equivalent fractions.

   $$\frac{1}{3} = \frac{}{9} \qquad \frac{5}{10} = \frac{}{20}$$

10. Label the points 2.8 and 3.4 on the number line.

    2.5   3.0   4.0

Exercise 28

1. About how long would it take to walk 4 miles, if you could walk 1 mile in 12 minutes?

_____ minutes

How many miles could you walk in one hour?

_____ miles

2. $(29 + 3) + 17 = 20 +$ _____

3. Put a < or > sign between each pair of fractions to show their relative value.

$$\frac{5}{12} \bigcirc \frac{3}{12}$$

$$\frac{7}{20} \bigcirc \frac{17}{20}$$

4. The temperatures for four days were:

Tuesday   0° C
Wednesday   15° C
Thursday   5° C
Friday   -5° C

Between which two days did the biggest change in temperature occur?

_____ to _____

5.
$$\begin{array}{r} 896 \\ \times\ 4 \\ \hline \end{array}$$
$$3\overline{)842}$$

6. Complete the pattern.

28, 32, ____, ____, ____

The rule is _____

7. List in order from **least to greatest**.

7.198   79.18   698.1   7.909

_____   _____   _____   _____

8. Fill in the missing fractions on the number line.

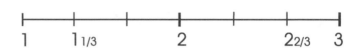

1   1 1/3   2   2 2/3   3

9. These balls are in the box.

Is it possible to pull out this combination?

❶ ④ ④ ④ ○

_____

10. Draw the polygons.

hexagon   scalene triangle

Exercise 29

1.  = $2.98    = $3.99

   How much money would you spend for two books and one pair of sandals?

   $ _____

....

2. Show one way of making $3.63 using coins and bills.

....

3. Find the sums and differences.

   $\dfrac{4}{25} + \dfrac{11}{25} =$ $\dfrac{4}{9} + \dfrac{5}{9} =$

   $\dfrac{7}{14} - \dfrac{5}{14} =$ $\dfrac{15}{16} - \dfrac{15}{16} =$

....

4. List the first five multiples of 6.

   ____ ____ ____ ____ ____

....

5. Finish the fact family.

   $72 \div 8 =$ ____

   _____

   _____

   _____

6. The bread recipe called for 5 cups of flour. One bag of flour holds about 10 cups. If you wanted to triple the recipe, how many bags of flour would you need to buy?

   ____ bags of flour

....

7. $(5 + 10) + 3 =$ ___ x ___

....

8. Fill in the missing numbers on the number line.

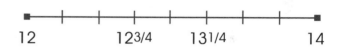

   12   12 3/4   13 1/4   14

....

9. School is over at 3:30 p.m. The choir concert starts at 7:15 p.m. How much time does Ben have between the time he gets out of school and the time he needs to be back for the concert?

   _____

....

10. $850 \div 10 =$ _____

   $853 \div 10 =$ _____

Exercise 30

1. Juan's car gets 30 miles per gallon of gas. How many miles can it travel on 8 gallons of gas?

   _____ miles

2. If Juan travels at 60 miles per hour for 2 hours, how many gallons of gas will he need?

   _____ gallons

3. What is this number?

   4 thousands + 2 hundreds + 7 ones + 1 ten

   a. 4,271   b. 4,712   c. 4,217

4.
   $$7,092$$
   $$-\,5,814$$

   $$77.6$$
   $$+\,8.92$$

5. Write fractions for points A and B on the number line.

6. Estimate and then solve.

   $$793$$
   $$\times\ 4$$

7. Round the prices to the nearest dollar and arrange in order of **least to greatest**.

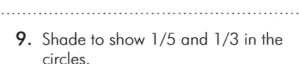

boat	doll	clown	book	truck
$3.89	$8.46	$4.28	$7.21	$5.29

   _____ _____ _____ _____ _____

8. If you had $20.00 to spend, what are two combinations of items you could buy?

   _____

   _____

9. Shade to show 1/5 and 1/3 in the circles.

10. Six times a number is 72. Write a number sentence that shows how to find the missing number. Solve the problem.

   _____

Exercise 31

Name _____

1. If a camel can walk 25 miles in one day, how far can it travel in 3 days?

   ____ miles

2. If a camel can travel for 6 days but then has to rest for 1 day, how many miles will the camel travel in 15 days?

   ____ miles

3.
   $\begin{array}{r}70\\ \times 9\\ \hline\end{array}$
   $\begin{array}{r}73\\ \times 9\\ \hline\end{array}$
   $\begin{array}{r}73\\ \times 10\\ \hline\end{array}$

4. $3 \times (7 + 2) =$ ____

5. Circle 2/7 of the octopuses.

   Circle 2/3 of the kangaroos.

   Circle 3/5 of the skunks.

6. Complete the pattern.

   730, 760, 790, _____, _____

7.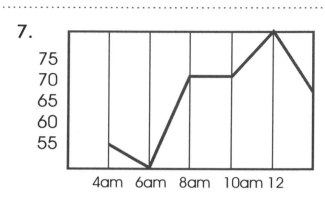

   During which time period was the largest increase in temperature?

   _____ to _____

8. Insert <, =, or > to make this a true number sentence.

   1793 ⬭ 1801

9. Locate and label the points 1.6, 1.8, and 2.3 on the number line.

   1 ├┼┼┼┼┼┼┼┼┼┼┼┼┼┼┼┼┤ 2

10. What time was it one hour and 30 minutes before the time shown on the clock?

    ____:____

Exercise 32

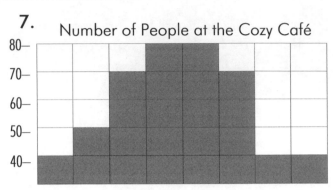

Name _____

1. A helicopter can travel 390 miles an hour. At that rate how far can it travel in 4 hours?

   _____ miles

2. Use front end estimation to round these numbers.

   66 _____   71 _____

   666 _____   710 _____

   6,710 _____   1,710 _____

3. Complete the pattern.

   113, 116, 115, 118, _____, _____

   The rule is _____

4.
860	867	867
×40	× 8	×38

5. What is the perimeter of this quadrilateral?

   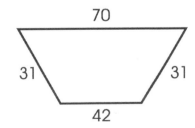

   _____ units

6. Insert <, =, or > to make this a true number sentence.

   179.29 ◯ 17.99

7. Number of People at the Cozy Café

   (bar graph with y-axis labeled 40, 50, 60, 70, 80 and x-axis labeled 8 am, 9 am, 10 am, 11 am, noon, 1 pm, 2 pm, 3 pm)

   At what time were there the most customers in the restaurant?

   _____ and _____

8. How many total customers did the restaurant have on this one day?

   _____ total customers

9. Which number sentence shows "7 times a number is 56"?

   7 × 56 = ☐   7 × ☐ = 56

   56 ÷ 7 = ☐

10. Locate and label 6.8 and 7.1 on the number line.

    (number line from 6 to 8)

Exercise 33

1. Randy ate 3 clusters of grapes. 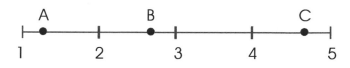 There were 21 grapes in each cluster. How many grapes did he eat?

____

2. Round these numbers to the nearest tenth.

71.29   .98   1.25

_____   _____   _____

3.
$$9 \times 3 \quad 9 \times 4 \quad 9 \times 5 \quad 9 \times 6 \quad 9 \times 7$$

4. Look at the answers to all the multiplication number sentences in question 3. When you add the digits of each product together what sum do you get?

> Example:
> 2 x 9 = 18 and 1 + 8 = ____

All the sums are ____.

5. Nolan bought a video game for $11.67. He gave the clerk a twenty dollar bill. How much change did he receive?

$_____

How much more money does he need to buy another game for $11.67?

$_____

6. Estimate the decimals for points A, B, and C.

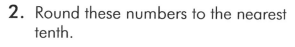

7. Continuing this pattern, how many peppers will be in the sixth row?

____

8.
$$400 \times 9 \qquad 405 \times 9 \qquad 425 \times 9$$

9. 7.8 + .29 + 31 + .5 = ____

10. Use mental math to solve.

40 + 70 + 60 + 30 + 10 + 90 = ___

Exercise 34

1. Karen went to the garage sale and bought 3 tools that cost $.77, $1.39, and $2.91. About how much money did she spend in all?

    a. $6.00   b. $5.00   c. $4.00

....

2. Jean wrote a 3 page poem with 17 lines on each page. How many lines did her poem have? _____

....

3. Tell how many sides these polygons have and how many congruent triangles will fit in a regular shape.

    hexagon - ____ sides   ____ triangles

    octagon - ____ sides   ____ triangles

    pentagon - ____ sides   ____ triangles

....

4. Write the multiplication and division fact family for the numbers 8, 9 and 72.

    _____

    _____

    _____

    _____

....

5. If this triangle is one fourth of the whole picture, what is the whole figure? Make a drawing. Name the shape.

6. This is how many people in the fourth grade have each kind of pet. Make a graph to show this information.

    bird |
    cat ||||| |||
    rabbit ||
    dog |||||

Fourth grade Pets

7. How many people are represented by the graph? _____

    How many more students own cats than dogs? _____

....

8. 867   867   8)743
   ×70   ×75

....

9. Mark the numbers 12.6 and 13.9 on the number line.

    ├┼┼┼┼┼┼┼┼┼┼┼┼┼┼┼┼┼┼┼┼┤
    12.0   13   14

....

10. Complete the pattern.

    420, 440, 460, ____, ____, ____

Exercise 35

Name _____

1. Steven had 5 packages of 300 baseball cards each. How many cards did he have?

   _____ cards in all

2. He is going to put these cards in an album that can hold 20 cards on each page. How many pages will he need to hold all of his cards?

   _____ pages

3. What is the area of the rectangle?

   3 m.

   7 m.

   area = _____ square meters

   What is the diameter of the largest circle that you could fit inside the rectangle?

   diameter = _____ meters

4. Draw a different rectangle that has the same perimeter as the rectangle above.

5.
7,000	7,193
−1,000	−927

6.  ☼ = 4 sunny days

   March ☼ ☼ ☼
   April   ☼ ☼ ☼ ☼
   May   ☼ ☼ ☼ ☼ ☼

   Shade and label the circle to make a graph that shows how many of the total sunny days were in each month.

   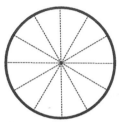

7. How many more sunny days were there in May than in April? _____

8. Which month was sunny about half of the time?

   _____

   Which month was sunny about two-thirds of the month?

   _____

9. 8.94 + 86.48 + .46 = _____

10. Write a decimal for the shaded part.

    _____
    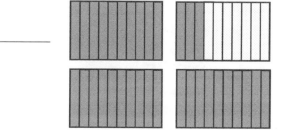

Exercise 36

1. Ben's rabbit had two litters of babies every year for ten years. If she had 60 babies in ten years, what was the average number of babies in each litter?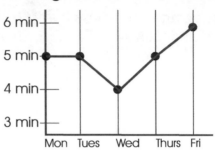

   _____ baby rabbits per litter

2. Draw lines and shade the rectangles below to show ⅔ and ¾.

   Which fraction is smaller? _____

3. $(15 + 29) + 31 = 15 + (29 + \underline{})$

4. If this rectangle is 4/3 of the whole, what would the whole be? Shade one whole.

   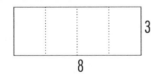

   8

   3

   What would be the length and width of one whole?

   l = _____   w = _____

5. Insert **<**, **=**, or **>** to make this a true number sentence.

   4.721 ⬭ 47.12

6. $4\overline{)400}$ $4\overline{)64}$ $4\overline{)464}$

Running Time for Half a Mile

6 min—
5 min—
4 min—
3 min—

Mon Tues Wed Thurs Fri

7. On which day did Erin run the half mile the fastest? _____

8. What is Erin's average time for the half mile? _____

9. Colors of Candy in the Bowl

red 10	green 30	yellow 29	brown 26

   Write a fraction to describe the probability of drawing each color.

   red _____   green _____

   yellow_____   brown_____

10.
   80
   ×78

   780
   × 8

   9,904,874
   − 387,681

Exercise 37

Name _____

1. If the fifth graders collected 3,527 cans in September, how many fewer was this than the 5,024 cans they collected in May?

_____ fewer cans

2. Jack has soccer practice in 2 hours and 20 minutes. It is 3:20 p.m. now. What time will he have practice? Show the time on the clock.

3. Finish the fact families.

$8 \div 2 = 4$ $240 \div 8 = 30$

_____   _____

_____   _____

_____   _____

4.
900	1000	967
×70	× 74	× 74

5. Find the perimeter.

P = _____

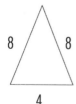

8   8

4

Draw a rectangle with the same perimeter.

6. Are these polygons congruent? _____

7. Write a decimal. _____

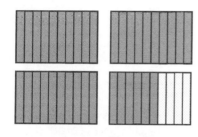

8. Write the name for these geometric solids.

_____   _____

9. Complete this chart.

Cost to Ride the Roller Coaster

rides	1	2	5	8	10
cost	$2.50				

10. In the standing long jump Mike jumped 1.3 meters and Ben jumped 1.7 meters. How much farther did Ben jump than Mike?

_____ meters

Exercise 38

1.

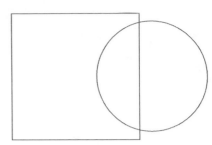

In the square write the set of numbers between 1 and 12 that are divisible by 2.

In the circle write the set of numbers between 1 and 10 that are divisible by 3.

What numbers are divisible by both 2 and 3? _____

Write these numbers in the area where the circle and square overlap.

2. $\frac{2}{3}$ of 30 = ____

3. Complete the pattern.

113, 109, 105, ____, ____

4. Write the fact family for 4, 60, and 240.

_____

_____

_____

_____

5. Find the sum and difference.

$\frac{3}{9} + \frac{5}{9} =$ $\frac{9}{12} - \frac{2}{12} =$

6.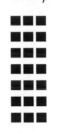

7. Write a multiplication problem for each array.

(___ × ___) + (___ × ___) = ___ × ___

8. Suzie is 65 inches tall. Billy is 5 feet tall. Who is taller and by how much?

_____ is _____ inches taller.

9. Write a number sentence that says, "A number times 50 is 200."

_____

10. Andrea has four coins in her wallet. What is the most amount of money she could have?

_____

If all the coins are different, what are two amounts of money she could have?

_____   _____

Exercise 39

1. If this is one third of the bags, how many bags are there altogether?

_____ bags

2. $\begin{array}{r} 168 \\ \times 76 \\ \hline \end{array}$ $8\overline{)99}$ $4\overline{)783}$

3. Megan ran 6 kilometers each day for 2 weeks. How many total kilometers did Megan run?

_____ kilometers

4. Write the number for:

32 ones + 11 tens + 1 hundred

_____

5. Jan has 6 coins that equal a dollar. What coins could she have?

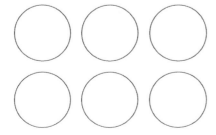

6. $9 \times 8 = (9 \times \underline{\quad}) + (9 \times \underline{\quad})$

7. $\begin{array}{r} 800,000 \\ -200,000 \\ \hline \end{array}$ $\begin{array}{r} 804,539 \\ -173,857 \\ \hline \end{array}$

8. Find the perimeter and the area of the square.

P = _____

A = _____

6 in.

Draw a different rectangle with the same area.

What is the perimeter of the new rectangle? _____

9. Write the first four multiples for:

12 _____

8 _____

10. Label the geometric figures.

_____   _____

Exercise 40

1. These are the prizes in the prize box.

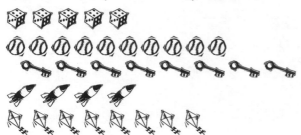

If you reached into the box what item would you be most likely to pull out?

_____

Write the fraction for the probability of pulling each item in the box.

2. 763,401   867,401
   – 34,777   +732,123

3. Round these numbers to the nearest hundred.

   567   3,542   100,497

   _____   _____   _____

4. 16 × 10 = ____

   16 × 12 = ____

5. 2 yards = ____ inches

   10 yards = ____ inches

6. Complete the patterns.

   710, 720, 730, 740, ____, ____

   740, 730, 720, ____, ____

7. Find the perimeter of the triangle.

   P = ____

Draw a rectangle with the same perimeter. What is its length and width?

8. Draw a line that is perpendicular to this line.

The angles are:
a. acute   b. right   c. obtuse

9. 16.3 + 7.53 = ____

10. Patrick wants to buy 38 pens. Pens are only sold in boxes of twelve. How many boxes does he need to buy?

   ____ boxes

Exercise 41

Name _____

1. Bob needs to make a pen for his sheep. He has 12 meters of fencing. Show all of the different pens he can make. Label the lengths and widths.

2. Write the number **thirty six thousand, four hundred six and eight tenths**.

   _____

3. $5.65 + $7.30 + $ .21 = _____

4. Label the numbers 3.7, 2.1, 3.2 and 2.6 on the number line.

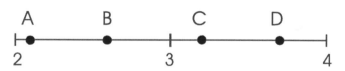

5. Find the sums.

   a. $\dfrac{2}{10} + \dfrac{5}{10} =$ ____

   b. .2 + .5 = ____

   c. $\dfrac{35}{100} + \dfrac{22}{100} =$ ____

   d. .35 + .22 = ____

6. Estimate the product before solving.

   $$\begin{array}{r} 86 \\ \times 47 \\ \hline \end{array}$$

7. Which of these angles are equal?

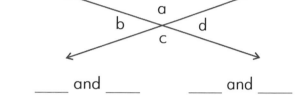

   ____ and ____   ____ and ____

8. Draw two parallel line segments. Draw a diagonal line that intersects both parallel line segments. Label the acute and obtuse angles.

9. Write these improper fractions as mixed numbers.

   $\dfrac{7}{4} =$ $\dfrac{13}{6} =$

10. Katie is 2 years younger than Ted. Ted is 4 years older than Matt. If Matt is 8 years old, how old are Katie and Ted?

    Katie_____   Ted_____

Exercise 42

1. Complete the table and then plot the points on the graph.

x	2	4	6	8	10
½ x	1			4	

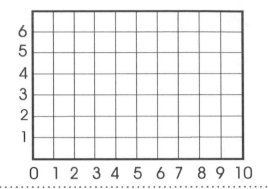

2. If this is 2/3 of the total number of presents Derek received for his birthday, how many presents did he receive?

_____ presents in all

3.
```
  7,000        7,000        7,004
 -3,500       - 3,523      +3,589
 _____       _____      _____
```

4.
```
  675          675          675
 ×  2         × 30         × 32
 ____         ____         ____
```

5. 750 × 3 = _____ = 10 × _____

6. Complete the pattern.

4, 2, 10, 8, 16, _____ , _____

The rule is _____

7.  = $105.50

 = $69.95

 = $45.95

What can you buy with $175.00?

_____

or _____

or _____

8. Jennifer has 4 friends. She gives each friend 4 friendship rings. How many friendship rings did Jennifer make if she also made 2 for herself?

_____ rings

9. Mrs. Watson gave her students 3 assignments. If she has 27 students, how many assignments does she have to grade?

_____ assignments

10. The top shelf of the bookcase has 10 books, the second shelf has 23 books, and the third shelf has 36 books. How many books are on the fifth shelf if this pattern continues?

_____ books

Exercise 43

Name _____

1. If you averaged 58 miles per hour on a 5-hour trip, what is the best estimate for the number of miles you would drive?

   a. 300   b. 12   c. 63

2. Julie has 2 coins in her wallet that are each less than 50¢. What are all the possible combinations of coins that she could have?

   _____   _____   _____

   _____   _____   _____

   _____   _____   _____

   _____

3.
   900,000   894,792
   −850,000   − 845,894

4.
   1.3   345.76
   + 6.53   − 40.6

5. 8)‾7,456   5)‾$45.65

6. This is the total number of sailboats in the race.

   Find the following fractions of the total number of boats.

   a. $\frac{7}{12}$ of the boats = ____ boats

   b. $\frac{2}{3}$ of the boats = ____ boats

   c. $\frac{5}{6}$ of the boats = ____ boats

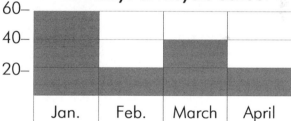

Birthdays at Meyers School

7. How many total birthdays are in these four months?

   ____ birthdays

8. Write a fraction to show the part of the birthdays that fall in each month.

   Jan. _____   Feb. _____

   March _____   April _____

9. How many more birthdays were in January than in April?

   ____ more birthdays

10. If this is one third of the students' birthdays for the entire year, how many students are at Meyers School?

    _____ students

Exercise 44

1. Two lots are for sale.
    lot 1 - 20 feet by 80 feet
    lot 2 - 40 feet by 50 feet
    Draw a picture to represent the two
    parcels of land and label each picture
    with the area and perimeter.

    lot 1   lot 2

    P = _____   P = _____

    A = _____   A = _____

    If the price for each lot was the same,
    which lot would you buy? _____

    Why? _____

2. 6 + (7+11) = ____ x ____

3.
    | 850 | 847 | 847 |
    | ×50 | × 7 | ×57 |

4. If this is 1/5 of all the cars in the parking
    lot, how many cars are there altogether?

    ____ cars altogether

5. 8)923   5)$65.80

6. 2 feet = _____ inches

    3 feet = _____ inches

    1 yard = _____ inches

    3 yards = _____ inches

7. Insert <, =, or > to make these true
    number sentences.

    5673 ◯ 578.5

    4732.5 ◯ 4732.9

8. Luis starts baseball practice at 3:30. He
    practices for 2 hours and 35 minutes.
    What time is it when he stops?

    ____:____ p.m.

9. Melody has 14 mice. Sam has 3 mice.
    All of them are in one cage. If you
    counted the legs on all of
    the mice, how many would
    there be?

    ____ legs

10. How many faces and vertices do these
    solid figures have?

    faces_____   faces_____

    vertices_____   vertices_____

Exercise 45

1. Sue drove 81 kilometers to Detroit, then 44 kilometers to Jacksonville. She took the same route home. About how many kilometers did she travel in all?

   _____ kilometers

2. Sue's car gets 25 kilometers per gallon. How many gallons did she use on this trip?

   a. 10   b. 25   c. 15

3. 1,700   1,693   8⟌720
   + 200   + 209

4. Complete the table.

T	2×T + 1
1	3
2	
3	
4	
5	

5. Insert <, =, or > to make these true number sentences.

   35.5 ◯ 30 $\frac{1}{4}$ + 5 $\frac{1}{4}$

   320.75 ◯ 500 − 170.5

6. The football team practiced 145 days this year. About how many months did they practice?

   a. 30   b. 4   c. 5

7. If the temperature is 45° on Thursday and it drops 50° on Friday, what will the temperature be on Friday? Show the temperature on the thermometer.

   _____ °

8. 804,975   45.55
   −535,820   −3.7

9. There are 4 six-packs in a case of soda cans. If you bought 2 cases, how many cans of soda would you have?

   _____ cans

10. 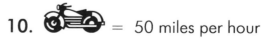 = 50 miles per hour

     = 10 miles per hour

    Marco is making a 150 mile journey. How much faster can he get there if he rides his motorcycles instead of his bicycle.

    _____ hours faster on the motorcycle

Exercise 46

1. Doughnuts are only sold in packages of a dozen. How many packages would you need for 450 people?

   _____ packages

   How many would be left over?

   _____ left over

2. For each doughnut you buy, you get 2 free doughnut holes. How many doughnuts and holes will you get if you buy 2 dozen doughnuts?

   _____ doughnuts and _____ holes

3. $4 + (12+3) = 5 +$ _____

   $(471 + 64) - 34 =$ _____

4. 3 yards = _____ feet

   6 yards = _____ feet

   9 yards = _____ feet

5. Find equivalent fractions.

   $\dfrac{4}{16} = \dfrac{}{4}$ $\dfrac{15}{30} = \dfrac{}{60}$

   $\dfrac{1}{5} = \dfrac{3}{}$ $\dfrac{1}{2} = \dfrac{}{20}$

6. Heather bought 6 dozen chocolate chip cookies. How many cookies did she buy? _____

   She ate 6 cookies. How many does she have left? _____

7.

   perimeter = _____ centimeters

   2 cm. / 6 cm.

   Draw a different rectangle with the same perimeter. Label the length and width.

8. Write the number for **six million, six hundred thirty and 4 hundredths**.

   _____

9. Name this geometric solid.

   _____

   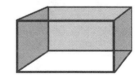

   How many faces does it have? _____

10. $\begin{array}{r} 814 \\ \times\ 60 \\ \hline \end{array}$ $\begin{array}{r} 814 \\ \times\ 64 \\ \hline \end{array}$ $7\overline{)4578}$

© Prufrock Press Inc. • Math Warm-Ups Grade 4

Exercise 47

1. Make a set of even numbers that have 5 in the hundreds place and 0 in the tens place.

   { ____ , ____ , ____ , ____ , ____ }

....

2. Name these polygons.

   _____   _____

....

3. Kenny practiced his saxophone for 540 minutes. How many hours did he practice?

   ____ hours

....

4. George's two cats had 6 babies each. Then each baby had 2 babies. How many cats are there now? Draw a diagram that shows your answer.

....

5. $\frac{3}{4}$ of $1.00 = ____

   $\frac{3}{4}$ of $4.00 = ____

6. Write the equivalent decimals.

   $\frac{5}{10}$ = .5 $\frac{8}{10}$ =

   $\frac{25}{100}$ = $\frac{75}{100}$ =

....

7. Find the perimeter.   P = ____ m.

   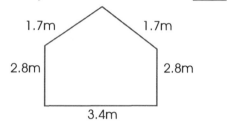

   1.7m   1.7m

   2.8m   2.8m

   3.4m

....

8. Paula has 16 bags that each have 2 ounces of candy. How many ounces of candy does she have?

   ____ ounces

....

9. Valerie bought 30 inches of blue lace and 18 inches of pink lace. How much lace did she buy in all?

   _____ inches, which equals _____ feet

....

10. What is the volume?

   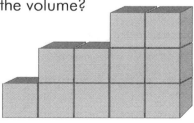

   ____ cubic units

Exercise 48

1. Roberto arrives at the bowling alley at 7:00. He bowls two games that take 45 minutes each to finish. What time will he finish bowling?

   ____:____

2. Round these numbers to the nearest ten thousand.

   69,450   113,758   936,312

   _____   _____   _____

3. Complete the table.

a	b	a × b
2		450
	150	450
5		450
10		450
	30	450

4. 300   309   6)3664
   × 40   × 40

5. Make a picture to show $\frac{1}{3}$ of 21.

6. 🧁 = 95¢   🥧 = 85¢   🍨 = $1.55

   If you bought 2 cupcakes, 2 pieces of pie and 1 ice cream, how much money would you spend? _____

   If you paid for this with one bill, what is the smallest bill that you could have used?

   _____

7. $5\frac{2}{7}$ $10\frac{5}{6}$
   $+3\frac{3}{7}$ $-4\frac{2}{6}$

8. 5,000   5,836   65.7
   − 431   + 712   3.8
                           +24.5

9. Complete the pattern.

   45.5, 42.5, 39.5, _____, _____

   The rule is _____

10. Estimate the sum before solving.

    34 + 148 + 71 + 389 + 16 = _____

    estimate
    ____ + ____ + ____ + ____ + ____

    estimate sum = _____

Exercise 49

1. The Wilson's bought a computer for $1,056.00 (including tax). They paid for it in six equal payments. How much was each payment?

   $_____

2. Insert <, =, or > to make these true number sentences.

   38.0 ◯ 83.0

   75.55 ◯ 75.54

   99.99 ◯ 99.990

3. Estimate before solving.

   784
   × 64
   _____

4. Max bought 3 gross of candy canes for $99 per gross. How much change did he get from $300.00?

   $_____

5. There are 144 candy canes in a gross. He gives a candy cane to each of the 389 students in his school. How many candy canes does he have left over?

   _____ left over

6. You have $15.00. You spent $4.50 on lunch, $6.50 for a movie and $3.50 for popcorn. How much money do you have left?

   $_____

7. Complete the patterns.

   20, 40, 80, _____, _____

   $\frac{1}{2}, \frac{1}{4}, \frac{1}{8}$, ___, ___

8. What is the perimeter of this rectangle?

   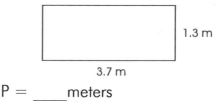

   1.3 m

   3.7 m

   P = _____ meters

9. Charlie bought 3 pounds 7 ounces of pecans and 5 pounds of sugar for making fudge. How many ounces of pecans did he buy?

   _____ ounces of pecans

10. If he used all of the sugar and all of the pecans to make fudge, what is the least amount the fudge could weigh?

    _____ pounds ___ ounces

Name _____

1. The price for a family membership at the swim club is $150. Individual child memberships are $75 each. If there are 3 children in a family, which is the most economical way to pay?

_____

2. Write in expanded notation.

   2,531 = _____ + _____ + _____ + _____

   Write the numeral for:
   6 tens + 4 thousands + 3 ones

   _____

3. 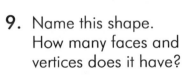 = 25¢   = 55¢   = 15¢

   How much would you have to spend for 10 pieces of paper, 5 file folders and 5 envelopes?

   $_____

4.
   3,784   3,784 $10.00
   × 90   × 94   − 6.39
   _____   _____   _____

5. Write each improper fraction as a mixed number.

   $\frac{8}{3}$ = $\frac{5}{2}$ =

6. $(50 + 16) + 3 = 3 \times$ ____

7. Write the set of **even** numbers greater than 244 and less than 257.

   { ___, ___, ___, ___, ___, ___, ___ }

8. This is 5/8 of the awards that will be given out on Track Day. How many total awards will be given out?

   ____ awards in all

9. Name this shape. How many faces and vertices does it have?

   _____   f = ___ v = ___

10. During the month Beth wrote checks for the following amounts:
    $7.35 $4.83 $10.50 $7.25.
    What is the best estimate for the total dollar amount of the checks that she wrote?

    about $_____

Exercise 51

Name _____

1. Nancy's school day is 6 hours and 30 minutes long. If she starts at 8:15 a.m., what time does she get out?

___:___

....

2. Write the decimals as fractions.

.2 =   .25 =   .05 =

....

3. These are the toys in the toy chest. If you reach in without looking, what is the probability of getting each toy?

tractor _____   helicopter _____

skateboard_____   car _____

....

4. Estimate before solving.

249
× 80
_____

....

5. Hans weighed 49.3 kilograms at the end of fourth grade. At the beginning of fifth grade he weighed 52.7 kilograms. How much weight did he gain?

_____ kilograms

6. What is the volume of this rectangular prism if
l = 6
w = 4
h = 3   V = _____ cubic units

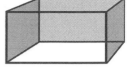

....

7.

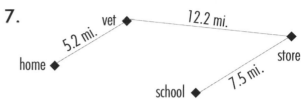

How many miles to drive from home to the veterinarian to the store and then to school?

_____ miles

....

8. Bill wants to buy 6 notebooks that cost 97¢ each. Estimate how much money he needs to buy the notebooks.

a. $6.00   b. $5.00   c. $7.00

....

9. Write the numeral for:
two hundred thirty-nine thousand, five hundred thirteen.

_____

....

10. If it is 85° today and the forecast is for 60° degrees tomorrow, how much colder will it be? _____°

Exercise 52

1. Ben went to the batting cages and hit 23 balls. Fred hit 3 times as many balls as Ben. How many balls did Fred hit?

   _____ balls

2. What is the perimeter of this rectangle?

   _____ in.

   If you enlarge this rectangle so that it is four times larger in length and width, what will the measurements be? What will the perimeter of the new, larger rectangle be?

   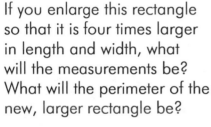

   4 in.

   8 in.

   l = _____   w = _____

   P = _____

3. List the factors for the numbers 40 and 64. Circle the common factors.

   40 _____

   64 _____

4. $\dfrac{5}{10} = \dfrac{}{100}$ $\dfrac{5}{10} = \dfrac{}{1000}$

5.
   ```
     300,000        468
   − 284,756      ×  73
   ```

6. This is 2/5 of the windsurfers in the race. How many windsurfers are there altogether?

   _____ windsurfers

7. Trey's bag of marbles weighed 3.6 kg. Jack's bag of marbles weighed 4.8 kg. Randy's bag weighed 2.9 kg. Estimate the total weight of all three bags.

   about _____ kilograms

8. Label the points 6.1, 6.8 and 7.5 on the number line.

   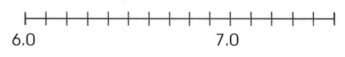

   6.0   7.0

9. Similar geometric figures are the same _____ but different _____.

10. The punch recipe uses 2 liters of soda, 1.5 liters of orange juice, and 1.5 liters of pineapple juice.
    How many liters of punch does the recipe make?

    _____ liters

© Prufrock Press Inc. • Math Warm-Ups Grade 4

Exercise 53

1. Write the minutes as fractional parts of an hour and in simplest terms.

60 minutes $= \dfrac{60}{60} =$ 1 whole

30 minutes $= \dfrac{}{60} = \dfrac{1}{}$

15 minutes $= \dfrac{}{60} = \dfrac{1}{}$

2. Write these amounts of money as fractional parts of a dollar.

$\$ .25 = \dfrac{}{4}$ $\$1.25 = 1\dfrac{}{4}$

$\$ .75 = \dfrac{}{4}$ $\$1.75 =$

$\$ .50 = \dfrac{}{2}$ $\$1.50 =$

3.   94,132   145,398
      − 5,047   +38,166

4.   409   70⟌486
       × 36

5. Angle ABC is an _____ angle.

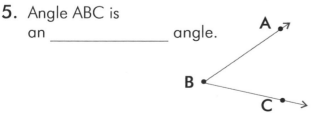

6. Write five multiples of 5 between 600 and 800.

_____ _____ _____ _____ _____

7. Locate and label the points 1.8, 1.3 and 1.5 on the number line.

1.0   1.7

8. Kylie has to divide 486 boxes of cookies among the six girls in her group. How many boxes will each girl get?

_____ boxes

Favorite Drinks

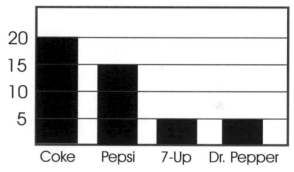

20
15
10
5

Coke Pepsi 7-Up Dr. Pepper

9. About how many more students chose Coke than 7-Up?

___ more chose Coke

10. About how many students are represented by the graph?

_____ students altogether

Exercise 54

1. Kyle had a job serving ice cream 5 days a week. He earned $10 more each day than the day before. He made $25.00 the first day. How much did he make on the seventh day?

day	amount earned
1	$25.00

2. Complete the pattern.

4, 9, 14, 19, ____, ____, ____

40, 90, 140, 190, ____, ____

3. 294.86
+62.307

Round your answer to the nearest whole number.

_____

4. 948
× 64

6)372

5. $\frac{3}{25} + \frac{9}{25} = \frac{}{25}$ $\frac{14}{15} - \frac{2}{15} = \frac{}{15}$

6. Jerome has $50.00 to spend on clothes. He buys a shirt for $14.35 and a pair of pants for $29.95. How much change should he get back?

$ _____

7. 905,842
−593,728

Round your answer to the nearest thousand.

_____

8. Arrange the numbers 22.75, 25.0, 22.5 and 25.5 from **smallest to greatest**.

_____ _____ _____ _____

9. What is the diameter of this circle?

d = ____

$r = 4\frac{1}{2}$

10. Carrie went shopping and purchased a sweat shirt for $6.95, sweat pants for $10.95, and sunglasses for $3.98. Taylor spent three times as much as Carrie did. About how much did Taylor spend?

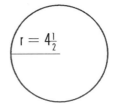

Taylor spent about $ _____.

Exercise 55

1. Parakeets come in yellow, blue, purple and green. If you buy a pair of parakeets, what are all the possible color combinations?

   _____ _____ _____

   _____ _____ _____

   _____

2. Insert <, =, or > to make each number sentence true.

   71.49 ◯ 79.49

   106.14 ◯ 106.04

   734.18 ◯ 73.418

3. Each  represents 5 kangaroos counted.

   Toby
   Jacob
   Jared

   How many kangaroos were counted altogether? _____

4. How many more kangaroos did Toby and Jacob count together than Jared counted?

   _____ more kangaroos

5. $4\frac{7}{8}$ $4\frac{4}{10}$
    $-2\frac{2}{8}$ $+5\frac{3}{10}$

6.   704,284   2,422
    − 472,874   +4,618

7. 840   850   847
    ×15   ×15   ×15

8. Find the least common multiple for the numbers 4 and 9.

   _____

   Find the least common denominator for the fractions 1/4 and 5/9.

   _____

9. The side of each square is 1 centimeter. What is the area and perimeter?

   A = _____
   P = _____

   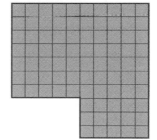

10. From Pittsburgh to Chicago is 471.4 miles. Akron is on the route between the two cities. It is 118.7 miles from Pittsburgh. How far is it from Akron to Chicago?

    _____ miles

Exercise 56

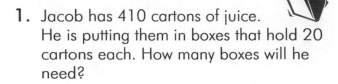

1. Jacob has 410 cartons of juice. He is putting them in boxes that hold 20 cartons each. How many boxes will he need?

_____ boxes

2. Draw two pentagons that are similar but not congruent.

3. How many minutes are in 1 hour and 30 minutes?

_____ minutes

A movie starts at 7:10 p.m. and is one and a half hours long. What time will it be when the movie is over?

___:___ p.m.

4. George bought 16 cans of beans for 30¢ each. How much would he save if he bought the beans at a store that sold them for 4 for $1.00?

$_____

5. Write the number **six thousand, forty-five and two hundredths**.

_____

6. Circle the largest fraction.

$\frac{3}{10}$ $\frac{4}{5}$ $\frac{3}{4}$ $\frac{3}{8}$

7. The dollar store sells everything for $1.00 or 50¢. Dade has $13.50 to spend. What is the least and the most number of items he could buy?

least _____   most _____

8. A x B = 3,600
What are three possible values for A and B?

A = ____   A = ____   A = ____
B = ____   B = ____   B = ____

9. Label the points 9.75 and 10.25 on the number line.

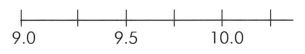

9.0   9.5   10.0

10. What is the perimeter of the polygon?

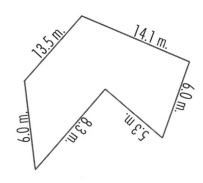

P = ____ meters

© Prufrock Press Inc. • Math Warm-Ups Grade 4

1. Ally has 200 pictures. Her photo album has 50 pages. Each page holds 6 pictures. How many blank pages will she have left after putting all of the photos in the album?

   ____ blank pages

2. Underline the thousands place in each number below and round the number to the nearest thousand.

   6,312,513   _____

   983,298   _____

3.
500	600	563
×76	×76	×76

4. 8)560   8)5600

5. Tina leaves school at 3:05 p.m. It takes her 25 minutes to walk to the recreation center. She takes an art class for 1 hour and 30 minutes and a drama class for 45 minutes. What time does she finish?

   ____:____ p.m.

6. This is 1/8 of the number of snowflakes that Cody cut out. How many snowflakes did he cut out altogether?
   ____ snowflakes

7. This is the amount of money each person in the scout troop collected.
   Milo - $4.55   James - $4.20
   Keith - $6.70   Gus - $7.15
   How much did they collect altogether?

   $_____

8. Circle the fraction that is equal to 1/2.

   $\frac{2}{8}$ $\frac{3}{4}$ $\frac{4}{8}$ $\frac{1}{4}$

   Which is the largest fraction? _____

9. Complete the pattern.

   245, 242, 239, _____, _____

10. Write fractions to show the parts of each array that are black.

    _____   _____

Exercise 58

1. P.J. is competing in the ten-mile marathon on the 31st. If he starts running on the third of October and runs 3 hours each day, how many hours will he have exercised by the end of the day on the 30th of October?

   _____ hours

2. If a = 8, what is:

   a + a + a + 5 = _____

3. Tommy ran 13 kilometers a day for 6 days and walked 2 kilometers a day for 16 days. How many kilometers did he walk and run altogether?

   _____ kilometers

4. Heather bought 5 dozen eggs. It takes 6 eggs to make an omelet. How many omelets can she make?

   _____ omelets

5. This is 3/8 of the kites that are flying. What is the total number of kites flying?

   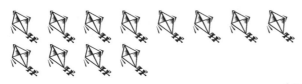

   _____ kites altogether

6. The zookeeper threw 36 fish to the seals. Later he threw 38 more fish. There are 6 fish still swimming with the seals. How many fish did the seals eat?

   They ate _____ fish.

7. Heidi buys five videos for $25.50 each. Her purchase was about:

   a. $150   **b.** $125   **c.** $175

8. $35.60
    ×   3
    _____

    4)$23.60

9. There are 13 tables in the cafeteria. There are 8 chairs at each table. How many tables must be added to seat 136 people?

   _____ more tables

10. Emily makes 6 valentines the first day and increases the number she makes each day by 7. How many days until she has made a total of 100 valentines?

day	1	2			
number made	6	13			
total					

Exercise 59

Name _____

1. Chad weighs 145 pounds. His mom weighs 35 pounds less than Chad. Chad's sister weighs 10 pounds less than her mom. How much more does Chad weigh than his sister?

____ pounds more

2. Complete the table.

S	7 × S + 2
1	9
2	16
3	
4	
5	

3. Write an equation that says "4 times a number is 76."

_____

4. If this line is two-thirds of a longer line, how long is the longer line?

____ inches

5. Write these decimals as fractions.

.7 = _____   .75 = _____

.075 = _____   .07 = _____

6. If the perimeter of a triangle is 28, what is the length of the missing side ?

____ cm.

7. 784   784   5)‾783‾
   ×60   ×63

8. Jill has 430 strawberry plants to plant in 5 strawberry beds. How many plants will be in each bed?

____ strawberries in each bed

9. Mrs. Turner had 5 classes of math. She had 27 students in each class. They each took 2 tests. How many tests did she have to grade?

____ tests

10. Write equivalent fractions.

$\frac{2}{7} = \frac{}{14}$ $\frac{3}{10} = \frac{}{40}$

Exercise 60

1. Caleb starts football practice at 11:15 a.m. and finishes 2½ hours later. When does he finish? Show the time on the clock.

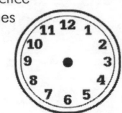

2. A car can travel 52 miles per hour. About how many miles can it travel in 12 hours?

   a. 500 mi.   b. 600 mi.   c. 700 mi.

3. Kathy and Matt shared a bag of sunflower seeds. Kathy ate .25 of the bag and Matt ate .40 of the bag.

   Who ate more ? _____

   How much more ? _____

4. This is how far Jason ran each day.

Mon.	Tues.	Wed.	Thurs.	Fri.	Sat.
4.7	6.7	9.7	13.7		

   How many more miles did he run on Wednesday than Tuesday? _____

   If this pattern continued, how many miles would he run on Saturday? _____

5. Round to the nearest tenth.

   5.67 _____   23.42 _____

   3.45 _____   12.15 _____

6. Write as improper fractions.

   $5\frac{1}{3} = \dfrac{}{3}$ $7\frac{1}{2} = \dfrac{}{2}$

7. $\dfrac{3}{13} + \dfrac{5}{13} =$ $\dfrac{12}{15} - \dfrac{7}{15} =$

8. Luke ran 784.75 meters, Jane ran 784.9 meters, Lily ran 713.28 meters, and Caleb ran 713.6 meters. Put the runners in order of who ran the most meters to who ran the least.

   _____   _____
       most

   _____   _____
                       least

9. 784
   × 74

   8)6436

10. Write decimals to show the part of the stars that are black and the part that are white.

    black = ____   white = ____

    ★★★★★★★★★★
    ★★★★★★★★★★
    ★★★★★★★★★★
    ★★★★★★★★★★
    ★★★★★★★★★★
    ★★★★★☆☆☆☆☆
    ☆☆☆☆☆☆☆☆☆☆
    ☆☆☆☆☆☆☆☆☆☆
    ☆☆☆☆☆☆☆☆☆☆
    ☆☆☆☆☆☆☆☆☆☆

Exercise 61

Name _____

1. Dan needs 1¾ hours to get ready and get to school. School starts at 8:00 a.m. What time does Dan need to wake up?

   ___:___

2. Complete the pattern.

   1, 6, 12, 19, ____, ____

   The rule is _____

3. Amy bought 2 pounds and 8 ounces of hamburger. How many ounces did she buy?

   ____ ounces

4. Jessica lives 3.5 kilometers from the park. Nicole lives 2.3 kilometers farther from the park than Jessica. How far does Nicole live from the park?

   ____ kilometers

5. The 4-H club needs a fence around a square garden. If one side of the garden is 26 meters, how much fencing will they need?

   ____ meters

6. Chad counted vehicles as they passed. Out of every 10 vehicles, 2 were trucks and the rest were cars. If this pattern continues what is the probability that the next vehicle that passes will be a car?

   Probability (car) = ___/10

7. Complete this chart to show how many cars and trucks he is likely to see.

cars	8				
trucks	2				
total	10	20	50	100	200

8. 1 meter = _____ centimeters

   $\frac{1}{5}$ meter = _____ centimeters

9. This is how many animals will be sold at the 4-H sale. How much money could be raised if all the animals are sold at the listed prices?

2	3	2
$45.00	$8.00	$10.50

   $ _____

10.
```
  4920        4920        4920
×    5      ×   20      ×   25
```

Exercise 62

Favorite Snacks

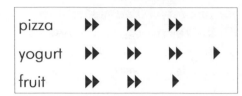

pizza	▸▸	▸▸	▸▸	
yogurt	▸▸	▸▸	▸▸	▸
fruit	▸▸	▸▸	▸	

each ▸▸ = 10 people

1. How many people are represented by this graph?

   ____ people

2. How many more people like yogurt than like fruit?

   ____ people

3. If x = 7 and y = 10, what is:

   x + x + y = ____

   y + y − x = ____

4. Carl planted .75 of his flower seeds in April and .25 in May. In which month did he plant more seeds?

   _____

5. Write a fraction that shows what part of the total amount of seeds he planted in May.

   ____

6.  = $5.95
    = $15.25
   🚀 = $17.95

   About how much would you spend if you bought all three items?

   a. $37.00   b. $38.00   c. $39.00

7. There were about 6,573 people at a concert. To the nearest hundred, estimate how many people were at the concert.

   _____

8. Write the numeral for **two hundred seventeen and five hundredths**.

   _____

9. Mrs. Green bought a rug on sale for $37.50. How much did she save if the original price of the rug was $50.00?

   $_____

10. 9 feet = ____ yards

    ____ cups = 1 pint

    ____ pints = 1 quart

    ____ quarts = 1 gallon

Exercise 63

1. List the factors for 63 and for 36. Circle the common factors of both numbers.

   63 _____

   36 _____

....

2. Put the fractions in order from least to greatest.

   $\dfrac{1}{10}, \dfrac{1}{8}, \dfrac{1}{12}$ _____

   $\dfrac{5}{12}, \dfrac{9}{12}, \dfrac{3}{12}$ _____

....

3. Mrs. Green planted 46 rows of corn with 30 plants in each row. How many corn plants did she have altogether?

   _____ corn plants altogether

....

4. $\begin{array}{r} 3,009 \\ \times\ 35 \\ \hline \end{array}$ $9\overline{)9843}$

....

5. From Washington to Jersey City is 223.6 miles. Philadelphia is somewhere between the two cities and is 137.2 miles from Washington. How far is Philadelphia from Jersey City?

   _____ miles

6. John ran 4.6 kilometers. Jamie ran 6.8 kilometers. How many more kilometers did Jamie run?

   _____ kilometers

....

7. Complete the table.

T	2	4	6	8	10
3T – 1	5				

....

8. Four students ran these distances in a 45-minute period:
   Nathan - 1.5 mi.   Briana - 1.9 mi.
   Sarah - 2.5 mi.   Mai Lee - 3.2 mi.
   How much farther was the combined distance of the two fastest runners than the combined distance of the two slowest runners?

   _____ miles farther

....

9. 6 grams = _____ milligrams

   600 millimeters = _____ centimeters

   2000 meters = _____ kilometers

....

10. ___ × 6 = 360

   10 × ___ = 360

Name _____

1. The Jimenez family owns five cars – red, yellow, white, black, tan. Only two cars can park in the garage. What are all of the possible combinations of cars that could be parked in the garage?

   _____ _____ _____

   _____ _____ _____

   _____ _____ _____

   _____

2. 469,345   1,000
   +748,569   –   8

3. 208   9)‾478‾
   ×63

4. Write the numbers that are 10,000 more than these numbers.

   23,550 _____

   4,108 _____

   675,350 _____

5. $(4 + 9) + 3 = 20 -$ ____

   $(4 + 9) \times 12 =$ ____

6. 6.30 meters = _____ centimeters

   6.30 meters = _____ millimeters

Most Popular Colors

blue	🕴🕴🕴🕴🕴🕴🕴🕴🕴
red	🕴🕴🕴🕴🕴
yellow	🕴🕴🕴🕴🕴🕴
purple	🕴🕴🕴🕴

🕴 = 5 people

7. How many more people liked blue than liked yellow? _____

   How many more people liked either red or yellow than liked purple? _____

8. How many people are represented by the data in the graph?

   _____

9. Write fractions to show the part of the whole that liked each color.

   blue = _____   red = _____

   yellow = _____   purple = _____

10. If a rectangle has a length of 40 centimeters and a width of 32 centimeters, what is the area?

    A = _____ sq. cm.

Exercise 65

Name _____

1. Mike is 6 feet 1 inch tall.
   Mindy is 5 feet 4 inches tall.
   How tall could Jill be, if she is taller than
   Mindy and at least 2 inches shorter than
   Mike? List all of the possibilities.

   _____

2. $4,090.03 $475.25
   – 2,915.34   +105.75

3. Four times a number is 80. Write an
   expression to find the missing number.

   _____

4. At school 29 children were
   each given a copy of the
   same reading book. Each
   book had 319 pages. If all
   29 children read every page,
   how many pages did they read?

   _____ pages altogether

5. $7.86   20)$138.80
   × 10

6. Paul earned $180.00 last summer
   mowing lawns. He bought a bicycle for
   $60.49. How much money did Paul
   have left over?

   $_____

7. 5 liters = _____ milliliters

   100 centimeters = _____ meters

8. Draw and label
   a radius and a
   diameter.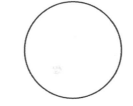

9. The Nyguen family took a trip from
   Chicago to St. Louis. They first drove
   125.4 miles to Champaign and then
   another 55.8 miles to St. Louis. What is
   the total distance they traveled from
   Chicago to St. Louis and back to
   Chicago?

   _____ miles

10. If each side of a regular
    hexagon is 14 centimeters,
    what is the perimeter?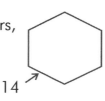

    14

    P = _____ centimeters

Exercise 66

Name _____

1. If a train travels at an average speed of 68 miles each hour, about how many miles will it travel in 12 hours?

    a. 800 mi.   **b.** 700 mi.   **c.** 900 mi.

2. Graph these points on the graph.
    (2,3) (3,4) (4,5) (5,6)

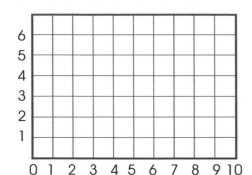

3. Add these fractions and write in simplest terms.

    $\frac{3}{8} + \frac{3}{8} =$ $\frac{3}{8} + \frac{6}{8} =$

4. Round these numbers to the nearest whole number.

    45.73   32.6   6.89   101.84

    _____ _____ _____ _____

5. 689
   × 57   20)1040

6. Continue the pattern.

    15, 20, 30, 45, ____, ____, ____

    The pattern is _____

7. 8,061   56,789
   −3,642   +19,689

8. faces = ____

   vertices = ____

   edges = ____

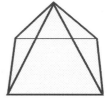

9. Sam is younger than Rachel and older than Jill. Write the names in order from oldest to youngest.

    _____ _____ _____
    oldest   youngest

10. What is the volume of a rectangular solid that has the following measurements?

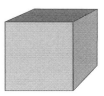

    l = 4   w = 8   h = 6

    V = ____ cubic units

    If you double the width, what will the volume be?

    V = ____ cubic units

Exercise 67

Soccer Goals Scored

Leticia	● ● ● ● ●
Damon	● ● ● ◗
Brooke	● ● ● ● ● ●
Sean	● ● ◗
Patrick	● ● ● ● ● ◗

● = 2 goals

1. How many goals were scored in all?

_____ goals

2. Which two players together scored a total of 12 goals? _____

3. What is the average number of goals scored by the five players?

_____

....

4. 496
   ×27

   6)546

....

5. If this is 2/5 of the magnets in the science classroom, how many magnets are there?

_____ magnets altogether

6. 7,000   300,425
   −2,689   +489,835

....

7. Estimate the number of miles you will drive during a 6 hour trip if you average 59 miles per hour.

about _____ miles

....

8. 85.93   45.45
   +7.8   −13.14

....

9. If 4 times a number is 76, what expression could be used to find the missing number? Solve.

_____

....

10. Draw each of these angles.

   right   obtuse   acute

Exercise 68

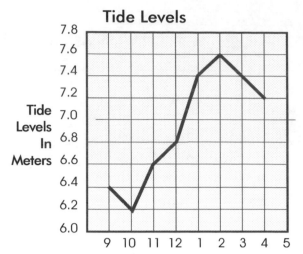

Tide Levels

Tide Levels In Meters

1. During which time period did the tide rise the most and by how much?

   _____   _____

2. At what time was the tide at the highest level? At what level was it?

   _____   _____

3.
   $$\begin{array}{r} 70.60 \\ -10.59 \\ \hline \end{array}$$

   $$\frac{45}{100} - \frac{13}{100} =$$

4. One package of stickers contains 32 sheets. There are 12 stickers on each sheet. How many stickers are in one package?

   ____ stickers

5.
   $$\begin{array}{r} 346 \\ \times 54 \\ \hline \end{array}$$

   $30\overline{)9330}$

6. What is the perimeter and area of this rectangle?

   P = ____

   A = ____

   32 m.

   96 m.

7. If you divide the rectangle into three equal parts, what will the area of each part be?

   A = ____

8. Complete the pattern.

   3, 6, 5, 8, 7, ____, ____, ____

   The rule is _____

9. A package contains 48 cookies. If there are 24 packages to a case, how many cookies are there in a case?

   ____ cookies

10. Laredo to Monterrey - 146 kilometers
    Monterrey to Mexico City - 600 km.
    Mexico City to Acapulco - 249 km.

    How many kilometers is the total trip from Laredo to Acapulco?

    _____ kilometers

Exercise 69

Name _____

1. Last Wednesday 75 children attended story time at the library. Each child checked out between 4 and 7 books each.

What is the least number of total books the children could have checked out?

_____

What is the greatest number of total books they could have checked out?

_____

2. Write the names of these polygons.

_____   _____

3. Erika and her 3 friends have 52 cards. If each girl gets an equal number of cards, how many cards will each girl get?

_____

4. Write the family of facts for 9, 80, 720.

_____   _____

_____   _____

5. Identify the angles as acute, right or obtuse.

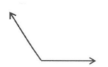

_____ _____ _____

6. Estimate the area of the polygon drawn on the grid.

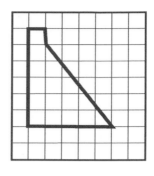

_____ sq. units

7. Write equivalent fractions.

$\dfrac{2}{3} = \dfrac{}{12}$ $\dfrac{7}{10} = \dfrac{56}{}$

$\dfrac{4}{8} = \dfrac{}{2}$ $\dfrac{3}{4} = \dfrac{9}{}$

8. Find the fraction of the whole.

$\dfrac{1}{2}$ of 16 = _____ $\dfrac{2}{3}$ of 15 = _____

$\dfrac{2}{10}$ of 100 = _____ $\dfrac{1}{4}$ of 100 = _____

9.
$$\begin{array}{r} 8{,}043.92 \\ -3{,}429.35 \\ \hline \end{array}$$
$$\begin{array}{r} \$12.50 \\ \times \quad 15 \\ \hline \end{array}$$

10. Write an equivalent decimal for each fraction.

$\dfrac{6}{10} = $ _____ $\dfrac{55}{100} = $ _____

Answers

Exercise 1, pg 5

1. 2
2. 7
3. 2, 7
4. 2 hours 20 minutes
5. >
6. 98,298
7. 8,840   253
8. 35,000   3,000
9. 105
10. football, tennis, volleyball, baseball

Exercise 2, pg. 6

1. a. equilateral
   b. scalene
   c. isoceles
2. 5 x 7 = 35   7 x 5 = 35
   35 ÷ 7 = 5   35 ÷ 5 = 7
3. 7/5   9/5
   rule - add 2/5
4. $3.90
5. 14, 21, 17
6. 88.73
7. 3,795   4,245
8. 30 or 3 tens
9. A = 35 units   P = 24 units
10. 359   13,610

Exercise 3, pg. 7

1. 1¼, 1¾, 2²⁄₄, 2¾
2. 8 triangles
3. 6   9   Alexa
4. 6 x 4 = 24   4 x 6 = 24
   24 ÷ 6 = 4   24 ÷ 4 = 6
   By knowing these facts, you just have to add a zero to the other problems.
5. 500   160   660
6. 480   90
7. $1.20 $1.80   30¢
   answers will vary
8. b. 249.17
9. 164,000   164,125
10. $3.92

Exercise 4, pg. 8

1. .25   .35   .50
2. all   a and c
3. 5/10 = 1/2
4. 11 hours
5. answers will vary, but some possible answers are:
   3 - $1.00 + 1 - 50¢
   2 - $1.00 + 3 - 50¢
   4 - 75¢ + 1 - 50¢
   3 - 75¢ + 2 - 50¢
6. >
7. 48,590   479,529
8. 21.09   72.48
9. 4,000   120   4,120
10.   4 × 4
   2 × 2 × 2 × 2

Exercise 5, pg. 9

1. 1 hour and 10 minutes
2. 1 hour
3. bus C   1/2 hour
4. rectangle   trapezoid
5. >   >   =
6. Jerry
7. 6,420   7,704
8. $100.06 $3.01
9. 1.89   1.99   2.01   2.10
10. 3,003
    1,506
    14,491
    158,034
    1,087

Exercise 6, pg. 10

1. 14
2. 5,000
3. Alex   1 cm.
4. shade circle to show 2/8
5. answers will vary but area of rectangle should equal 24
6. 1,611   10,121
7. 21   28
8. 13,160   13,000
9. 8:20
10. $7,000

Exercise 7, pg.11

1. 150   200   250
2. 31, 38, 45
   rule - add 7
3. 4
4. 1,704   163
5. 5.2, 5.3, 5.5
6. 18 pages
7. pentagon with a line of symmetry
8. 4000 + 300 + 10 + 2
9. 49 r1   172,385
10. Thomas - 12   James - 22
    Jill - 122   Brad - 160

Exercise 8, pg. 12

1. 47,000
2. Carrie has more
3. 558   620   682
4. A = 22
5. 4.2
6. .26
7. 100 ml.
8. 20 people
9. 61, 63, 65, 67, 69
10. 583,197   50,917

Exercise 9, pg. 13

1. 220 miles
2. 9.0   42.4 $4.73
3. 68,409   57
4. 1⅓ pizzas for each person
5. $22.50
6. 3 2 1 0
   10 5 0 5
   10 0 5 5
7. 513,455
8. 54,000   57,152
9. A H I M O T U V W X Y
10. 15 min.

Exercise 10, pg. 14

1. 82, 84, 86, 88
2. 9,000   4,500   13,680
3. The third problem is sum of the first two problems.
   210
4. 7
5. $9 \times 4 = 36$ $4 \times 9 = 36$
   $36 \div 9 = 4$ $36 \div 4 = 9$
   360   360   3,600
6. array to show
   $(2 \times 7) + (3 \times 7) = 5 \times 7$
7. yes, $3.30 left over
8. 1.14
9. .45 gardenias
   1.23 cacti
   3.6 sunflowers
   6.2 palm
10.

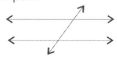

Exercise 11, pg. 15

1. Matt
2. 769   2,208
3. 1,272   estimate - 1,300
4. $3 \times \square = 18$
5. 2   2½   6
6. .5   5/10
7. 62,720   5,376   68,096
8. Central St.
   Maple St.
9. Michigan Ave.
10. Maple St.

Exercise 12, pg. 16

1. graph to show:
   A - 320,000
   B - 330,000
   C - 300,000
2. 642,001, 642,003
   642,005, 642,007
3. 100   100
   200   300
   1,200   1,200
4. 476   45 r5
5. 15, 12, 9
6. $2.99 $13.51 $2.29
7. answers will vary
8. 4.263   8.642   14.29   41.99
9. <
10. 30.5 sq. meters

Exercise 13. pg. 17

1. 94
2. a. 35
3. 4
4. 360 minutes $60.00
5. $4.10 $62.45
6. 24.72
7. 2.892   6.901   36.25   645.8
8. 46,400   52,200   51,852
9. correctly drawn graph
10. 4:00 p.m.

Exercise 14, pg. 18

1. 80   90
2. 5/7   6/15 or 2/5
3. $(6 \times 4) + (6 \times 3) = 42$
4. 256,510   449,798
5. clock should show 12:00
6. correctly drawn diagonals
7. 188, 183
   rule - subtract 1, 2, 3, 4 ...
8. estimate - 450
   actual - 464
9. points correctly located on number line
10. 3.3

Exercise 15, pg. 19

1. 1.9 2.04 2.14 2.4
2. hexagon with lines of symmetry
3. 4 hours
4. 2,000   2,355   2,500
5. 7,610   448,655
6. 1,000   2,000   4,000
7. Sept 5th
8. Sept 8th, 10th, 22th, and 24th
9. Oct 1st
10. 5/25 or 1/5
    12/20 or 3/5

Exercise 16, pg. 20

1. possible answers are:
   1×17 2×16 3×15
   4×14 9×9 5×13
   6×12 7×11 8×10
2. possible answers are:
   17   32   45   56
   81   65   72   77   80
3. the rectangle with the largest area
4. the rectangle with the longest length and shortest width
5. 151, 142, 133
   rule - subtract 9
6. 60   120   150   300
7. >
8. 2.32
9. 3330, 3332, 3334, 3336, 3338
10. 1.8

Exercise 17, pg. 21

1. 19,643
2. $8,000 $8,000 $10,400
3. 1,400,082   147,778
4. 4/8   4/12
5. 81, 72, 63, 54
   rule - subtract 9
6. $1,100.00
7. answers will vary
8. O = 5/16   ● = 3/16
   ◎ = 8/16
9. 5/7   9/12 or 3/4
10. sphere   cube
    0 faces   6 faces

Exercise 18, pg. 22

1. $14.50
2. 3/8   4/10 or 2/5
   2/6 or 1/3
3. $6 \times 7 = 42$ $7 \times 6 = 42$
   $42 \div 6 = 7$ $42 \div 7 = 6$

   $9 \times 6 = 54$ $54 \div 6 = 9$
   $6 \times 9 = 54$ $54 \div 9 = 6$
4. 2
5. Randy 3/4 < 4/5
6. 20   2,625   5,250
7. 39   53   67   81   95
8. clock shows 3:55 p.m.
9. 30   29 r1
10. 1, 548

Exercise 19, pg. 23

1. 13,000 18,000 156,000
2. triangular prism pyramid
3. 54
4. 4,926, 4,296, 3,151, 2,968
5. 3,051 3,451
6. circle divided and labeled correctly
7. 55 58 r3 550
8. 1,903 2,193
9. shade 4 4/12
10. John, Rex, Raul and Bill

Exercise 20, pg. 24

1. A = $7\frac{2}{10}$ B = $7\frac{9}{10}$
   C = $8\frac{3}{10}$
2. 3 x □ = 210
3. 1,277 2,635
4. 1,413 2,826
5. 5 5/40 or 1/8
6. <
7. shade 3/5 and 7/10; Buzz
8. Suzanne $1.35
9. 4:00 p.m.
10. 2.6

Exercise 21, pg. 25

1. 2,067,337
2. 81
3. 78
4. $18
5. $169.49 568
6. 15 66 56
7. 585 about 12 hours
8. 54,000 55,062 215 r2
9. 6 in.
10. 48

Exercise 22, pg. 26

1. $6,260,000
2. 194 minutes
3. 7:15
4. 6,856 300
5. > = <
6. 5 10
7. 85
8. armadillo = 120
   rabbit = 150
   racoon = 150 fox = 90
9. 19 and 23
10. (9 x 7) – (5 x 7)

Exercise 23, pg. 27

1. 154 107 308
2. 111 333
3. 39, 45
   rule - add 8, add 6
4. 9.7 1.5 386.2
5. 368,227 62,580
6. D and B A and C
7. 3 hours 6 p.m.
8. correctly shaded circle
   2/4
9. 10 x □ = 90
   or 90 ÷ □ = 10
10. 3

Exercise 24, pg. 28

1. 40 sandwiches
2. drawings of triangle, parallelogram and rhombus
3. 1,401 462,991
4. $18\frac{4}{6}$ $22\frac{5}{6}$ $26\frac{6}{6}$ or 27
   rule - add $4\frac{1}{6}$
5. 2,800 12,800 200
6. 4 x 4 16 x 1 2 x 8
7. 1 - $1.00 1 - $5.00 4 - 5¢
8. shade to show 64°
9. $\frac{1}{5}$ $\frac{3}{10}$ $\frac{6}{10}$ $\frac{4}{5}$
10. 6.2 6.6 7.1

Exercise 25, pg. 29

1. 1,500
2. 5 min. 10 min
3. 419,492.5
4. $37.00
5. 5.2 5.9 6.5
6. A = 12 sq. cm.
   P = 14 cm.
   answers will vary
7. 20,488 19,926 87 r3
8. 400 444.993
9. .2 .6
10. 11
    35
    161
    857
    4,240

Exercise 26, pg. 30

1. 10 20 25 5
2. 15
3. 89 88 88
4. 112
5. 36.62 $269.67
6. 14,000 15,048 117 r6
7. 100,000 116,127
8. > <
9. 24
10. Mary $2.00

Exercise 27, pg. 31

1. 4
2. $4.00
3. 2,150 2,148 r1
4. b. 20 x 3
5. $18.75
6. 20.678 9.005
7. 21
8. < = >
9. 3/9 10/20
10. correctly label 2.8 and 3.4

Exercise 28, pg. 32

1. 48 min. 5 mi.
2. 29
3. > <
4. Tuesday - Wednesday
5. 3,584 280 r2
6. 36, 40, 44,
   rule - add 4
7. 7.198 7.909 79.18 698.1
8. $1\frac{2}{3}$ $2\frac{1}{3}$
9. yes
10. drawing of a hexagon and scalene triangle

Exercise 29, pg. 33

1. $10.96
2. answers will vary
3. 15/25 9/9 or 1
   2/14 0/16 or 0
4. 6, 12, 18, 24, 30
5. 72 ÷ 8 = 9 72 ÷ 9 = 8
   8 x 9 = 72 9 x 8 = 72
6. 2 bags
7. 3 x 6 or 2 x 9 or 1 x 18
8. $12\frac{1}{4}$ $12\frac{2}{4}$ 13 $13\frac{2}{4}$ $13\frac{3}{4}$
9. 3 hours 45 minutes
10. 85 85 r3

Exercise 30, pg. 34
1. 240 miles
2. 4 gallons
3. c. 4,217
4. 1,278   86.52
5. 1⅔   1⅚
6. 3,200   3,172
7. boat $4   clown $4
   truck $5   book - $7
   doll $8
8. answers will vary
9. correctly shaded circle
10. 6 x □ = 72
    or 72 ÷ □ = 6
    c = 12

Exercise 31, pg. 35
1. 75 miles
2. 325 miles
3. 630   657   730
4. 27
5. circle 4 octopuses
   circle 4 kangaroos
   circle 9 skunks
6. 820   850
7. 6 a.m. to 8 p.m.
8. <
9. label points 1.6, 1.8, and 2.3
10. 9:30

Exercise 32, pg. 36
1. 1,560 miles
2. 70   70
   700   700
   7,000   2,000
3. 117, 120
   rule - add 3, subtract 1
4. 34,400   6,936   32,946
5. 174 units
6. >
7. 11 a.m. and noon
8. 470
9. 7 x □ = 56
10. label points 6.8 and 7.1

Exercise 33, pg. 37
1. 63
2. 71.3   1.0   1.3
3. 27, 36, 45, 54, 63
4. 9
5. $8.33 $3.34
6. A = 1.3   B = 2.7   C = 4.7
7. 13
8. 3,600   3,645   3,825
9. 39.59
10. 300

Exercise 34, pg. 38
1. b. $5.00
2. 51
3. hexagon - 6   6
   octagon - 8   8
   pentagon - 5   5
4. 8 x 9 = 72   9 x 8 = 72
   72 ÷ 8 = 9   72 ÷ 9 = 8
5. a quadrilateral that
   incorporates four of the given
   triangle
6. correctly shaded graph
   bird - 1
   cat - 8
   rabbit - 2
   dog - 5
7. 16   3
8. 60,690   65,025   92 r7
9. correctly label 12.6 and 13.9
10. 480, 500, 520

Exercise 35, pg. 39
1. 1,500 cards
2. 75 pages
3. 21 sq. m.   3 m.
4. rectangle should have P = 20
5. 6,000   6,266
6. correctly labeled circle graph
   March - 3 sections shaded
   April - 4 sections shaded
   May - 5 sections shaded
7. 4
8. April   May
9. 95.88
10. 3.3

Exercise 36, pg. 40
1. 3
2. rectangle correctly shaded; 2/3
3. 31
4. shade 3 sections
   l = 6   w = 3
5. <
6. 100   16   116
7. Wednesday
8. 5 minutes
9. red = 10/95
   green = 30/95
   yellow = 29/95
   orange = 26/95
10. 6,240   6,240   9,517,193

Exercise 37, pg. 41
1. 1,497
2. clock showing 5:40 p.m.
3. 8 ÷ 4 = 2   240 ÷ 30 = 8
   4 x 2 = 8   30 x 8 = 240
   2 x 4 = 8   8 x 30 = 240
4. 63,000   74,000   71,558
5. 20
6. no
7. 3.6
8. pyramid   sphere
9. $5.00 $12.50
   $20.00 $25.00
10. .4 meters

Exercise 38, pg. 42
1. square - 2, 4, 6, 8, 10
   circle - 3, 6, 9
   common - 6
2. 20
3. 101, 97
4. 60 x 4 = 240   4 x 60 = 240
   240 ÷ 60 = 4   240 ÷ 4 = 60
5. 8/9   7/12
6. 54,000   55,936   90
7. (7 x 3) + (7 x 2) = 7 x 5
8. Susie   5"
9. □ x 50 = 200
10. $4.00; answers will vary

Exercise 39, pg. 43

1. 36
2. 12,768   12 r3   195 r3
3. 84 kilometers
4. 242
5. 3 - 25¢   2 - 10¢   1 - 5¢
6. answers will vary; sum of the factors should be 8
7. 600,000   630,682
8. P = 24 in.   A = 36 sq. in.
   answers will vary
9. 12   24   36   48
   8   16   24   32
10. trapezoid   parallelogram

Exercise 40, pg. 44

1. ball
   dice - 5/35   ball - 10/35
   key - 8/35   rocket - 4/35
   kite - 8/35
2. 728, 624   1,599,524
3. 600   3,500   100,500
4. 160   192
5. 72   360
6. 750, 760
   710, 700
7. 24; answers will vary
8. correct drawing   b. right
9. 23.83
10. 4

Exercise 41, pg. 45

1. 3 x 3   2 x 4   1 x 5
2. 36,406.08
3. $13.16
4. A = 2.1   B = 2.6
   C = 3.2   D = 3.7
5. 7/10   .7
   57/100   .57
6. 4,500   4,042
7. a and c   b and d
8. drawing as directed

   Angles labeled **a** are acute.
   Angles labeled **b** are obtuse.
9. 1¾   2⅙
10. Ted = 12   Kate = 10

Exercise 42, pg. 46

1. 2   4   6   8   10
   1   2   3   4   5
   correctly plotted points will make a straight line
2. 9
3. 3,500   3,477   10,593
4. 1,350   20,250   21,600
5. 2,250   10 x 225
6. 14, 22
   rule - subtract 2, add 8
7. answers will vary
8. 18
9. 81
10. 62

Exercise 43, pg. 47

1. a. 300 miles
2. pp   nn   dd
   pn   nd   dq
   pd   nq   qq
   pq
3. 50,000   48,898
4. 7.83   305.16
5. 932 $9.13
6. 7   8   10
7. 140
8. Jan. - 60/140
   Feb. - 20/140
   March - 40/140
   April - 20/140
9. 40
10. 420

Exercise 44, pg. 48

1. lot 1
   P = 200   A = 1600
   Lot 2
   P = 180   A = 2000
   Lot 2 - You get more land for your money.
2. 6 x 4 or 2 x 12 or
   1 x 24 or 3 x 8
3. 42,500   5,929   48,279
4. 40
5. 115 r3 $13.16
6. 24   36
   36   108
7. >   <
8. 6:05
9. 68
10. cube   pyramid
    f = 6   f = 4
    v = 8   v = 4

Exercise 45, pg. 49

1. 250
2. a. 10
3. 1,900   1,902   90
4. 5   7   9   11
5. =   <
6. c. 5
7. -5°
8. 269,155   41.85
9. 48
10. 12 hours

Exercise 46, pg 50

1. 38 packages   6 left over
2. 24 doughnuts and 48 holes
3. 14   501
4. 9   18   27
5. 1/4   30/60
   3/15   10/20
6. 72   66
7. 16 cm; answers will vary
8. 6,000,630.04
9. rectangular prism   6
10. 48,840   52,096   654

Exercise 47, pg 51

1. 500   502   504   506   508
2. hexagon pentagon
3. 9 hours
4. 38
5. 75¢ or $.75
   $3.00
6. .8   .25   .75
7. 12.4
8. 32 ounces
9. 48 inches = 4 feet
10. 11

Exercises 48, pg. 52

1. 8:30
2. 70,00   110,000   940,000
3. 2 x 225
   3 x 150
   5 x 90
   10 x 45
   15 x 30
4. 12,000   12,360   610r4
5. picture of 21 objects with 7 circled or shaded
6. $5.15 $10.00
7. 8 5/7   6 3/6 or 6 1/2
8. 4,569   6,548   94.0
9. 36.5   33.5
   rule - subtract 3
10. actual sum = 658
    30 + 150 + 70 + 390 + 20
    estimate sum = 660

Exercise 49, pg. 53

1. $176.00
2. <   >   =
3. 48,000   50,176
4. $3.00
5. 43
6. $. 50
7. 160   320
   1/16   1/32
8. 10 m.
9. 55 ounces
10. 8 pounds 7 ounces

Exercise 50, pg. 54

1. $150.00 - family price
2. 2000 + 500 + 30 + 1
   4,063
3. $6.00
4. 340,560   355,696
   $3.61
5. 2 2/3   2 1/2
6. 23
7. 246, 248, 250, 252, 254, 256
8. 16
9. cylinder f = 3   v = 0
10. $30.00

Exercise 51, pg. 55

1. 2:45 p.m.
2. 2/10   25/100   5/100
3. tractor 1/10
   helicopter - 3/10
   skateboard - 2/10
   car - 4/10
4. 20,000   19,920
5. 3.4 kg
6. 72
7. 24.9 miles
8. a. $6.00
9. 239,513
10. 15°

Exercise 52, pg. 56

1. 69 balls
2. 24 in.
   l = 32   w = 16   P = 96
3. 40 - 1, 2, 4, 5, 8, 10, 20, 40
   64 - 1, 2, 4, 8, 16, 32, 64
   common - 1, 2, 4, 8
4. 50/100   500/1000
5. 15,244   34,164
6. 20
7. 11 kg.
8. numbers correctly labeled
9. same shape but different size
10. 5 liters

Exercise 53, pg. 57

1. 30/60 = 1/2
   15/60 = 1/4
2. .25 = 1/4 $1.25 = 1 1/4
   .75 = 3/4 $1.75 = 1 3/4
   .50 = 1/2 $1.50 = 1 1/2
3. 89,085   183,564
4. 14, 724   6 r66
5. acute
6. answers will vary; multiples of 5
7. correctly labeled points
8. 81
9. 15
10. 45

Exercise 54, pg. 58

1. 1 - $25   5 - $65
   2 - $35   6 - $75
   3 - $45   7 - $85
   4 - $55
   $85
2. 24, 29, 34
   240, 290
3. 357.167 357
4. 60,672 62
5. 12/25   12/15
6. $5.70
7. 312,114   312,000
8. 22.5   22.75   25.0   25.5
9. 9
10. $66

Exercise 55, pg. 59

1. yy   bb   pp
   yb   bp   pg
   yp   bg   gg
   yg
2. <   >   >
3. 80
4. 10
5. 2 5/8   9 7/10
6. 231,410   7,040
7. 12,600   12,750   12,705
8. 36   36
9. P = 40   A = 85
10. 352.7 miles

Exercise 56, pg. 60

1. 21 boxes
2. two similar pentagons
3. 90 min.   8:40 p.m.
4. 80¢
5. 6,045.02
6. 4/5
7. least - 14   most - 27
8. possible answers are:
   2x1800   3x1200   4x900
   5x720   6x600   8x450
   9x400   10x360   12x300
   60x60   3600x1   30x120
   20x180   200x18   90x40
9. correctly labeled points on number line
10. 53.2 m.

Exercise 57, pg. 61

1. 16 pages
2. 6,313,000   983,000
3. 38,000   45,600   42,788
4. 70   700
5. 5:45 p.m.
6. 104
7. $22.60
8. 4/8   3/4
9. 236, 233
10. 14/21 or 2/3   8/24 or 1/3

Exercise 58, pg. 62

1. 84
2. 29
3. 110 kilometers
4. 10
5. 32
6. 68
7. b. 125
8. $106.80 $5.90
9. 4 more tables
10. 6   13   20   27   34
    6   19   39   66   100
    the fifth day

Exercise 59, pg. 63

1. 45 pounds
2. 23   30   37
3. 4 x □ = 76
4. 3 inches
5. 7/10   75/100
    75/1000   7/100
6. 13 cm.
7. 47,040   49,392   156 r 3
8. 86
9. 270 tests
10. 4/14   12/40

Page 60, pg. 64

1. 1:45 p.m.
2. b. 600 mi.
3. Matt   .15
4. 3.0   24.7
5. 5.7   23.4
    3.5   12.2
6. 16/3   15/2
7. 8/13   5/15 or 1/3
8. Jane - 784.9   Luke - 784.75
    Caleb - 713.6   Lily - 713.28
9. 58,016   804 r4
10. b = .55   w = .45

Exercise 61, pg. 65

1. 6:15 am
2. 27, 36
    rule - add 5, add 6, add 7 ...
3. 40 oz.
4. 5.8 km.
5. 104 m.
6. 8/10
7. 8   16   40   80   160
   2   4   10   20   40
  10   20   50   100   200
8. 100   20
9. $135
10. 24,600   98,400   123,000

Exercise 62, pg. 66

1. 90
2. 10
3. 24   13
4. April
5. 1/4 or 25/100
6. c. $39.00
7. 6,600
8. 217.05
9. $12.50
10. 9 feet = 3 yards
    2 cups = 1 pint
    2 pints = 1 quart
    4 quarts = 1 gallon

Exercise 63, pg. 67

1. 63 - 1, 3, 7, 9, 21, 63
    36 - 1, 2, 3, 4, 6, 9, 12,
       18, 36
    common - 1, 3, 9
2. 1/12   1/10   1/8
    3/12   5/12   9/12
3. 1,380
4. 105,315   1093 r6
5. 86.4 mi.
6. 2.2 km.
7. 11   17   23   29
8. 2.3 mi.
9. 6000 mg   60 cm   2 km
10. 60   36

Exercise 64, pg. 68

1. ry   yw   wb
    rw   yb   wt
    rb   yt   bt
    rt
2. 1,217,914   992
3. 13,104   53 r1
4. 24,550   5,108   676,350
5. 4   156
6. 630 cm.   6,300 mm.
7. 15   45
8. 150 people
9. b - 55/150   r - 30/150
    y - 40/150   p - 25/150
10. 1,280 sq. cm.

Exercise 65, pg. 69

1. 5'11", 5'10", 5'9", 5'8", 5'7",
    5'6", or 5'5"
2. $1,174.69 $581.00
3. 4 x □ = 80
    □ = 20
4. 9,251 pages
5. $78.60 $6.94
6. $119.51
7. 5,000 ml.   1 m.
8. correctly drawn radius and
    diameter
9. 362.4 miles
10. 84 cm.

Exercise 66, pg. 70

1. a. 800
2. points correctly graphed will
    form a straight line
3. 6/8   9/8 = $1\frac{1}{8}$
4. 46   33   7   102
5. 39,273   52
6. 65   90   120
    rule - add 5, add 10, add 15...
7. 4,419   76,478
8. f - 5   v - 5   e - 8
9. Rachel   Sam   Jill
10. 192   384

Exercise 67, pg. 71

1. 45 goals
2. Damon and Sean
3. 9
4. 13,392 91
5. 20
6. 4,311 790,260
7. 360 miles
8. 93.73 32.31
9. 4 x B = 76 B = 19
10. right obtuse acute

Exercise 68, pg. 72

1. 12 to 1 .6 m.
2. 2:00 7.6 m.
3. 60.01 32/100 = 8/25
4. 384 stickers
5. 18,684 311
6. P = 256 m.
 A = 3,072 cubic meters
7. 1,024 cubic meters
8. 10, 9, 12
 rule - add 3, subtract 1
9. 1,152 cookies
10. 995 km.

Exercise 69, pg. 73

1. 300 books 525 books
2. parallelogram trapezoid
3. 13
4. 9 x 80 = 720
 80 x 9 = 720
 720 ÷ 80 = 9
 720 ÷ 9 = 80
5. obtuse acute right
6. 15 - 16 square units
7. 8/12 56/80
 1/2 9/12
8. 8 10
 20 25
9. 4,614.57 $187.50
10. .6 .55

Math Warm-Ups (Grade 4)

All lessons in this book align to the following standards.

Grade Level	Common Core State Standards in Math
Grade 4	4.OA.A Use the four operations with whole numbers to solve problems. 4.OA.B Gain familiarity with factors and multiples. 4.OA.C Generate and analyze patterns. 4.NBT.A Generalize place value understanding for multi-digit whole numbers. 4.NBT.B Use place value understanding and properties of operations to perform multi-digit arithmetic. 4.NF.A Extend understanding of fraction equivalence and ordering. 4.NF.B Build fractions from unit fractions. 4.NF.C Understand decimal notation for fractions, and compare decimal fractions. 4.MD.A Solve problems involving measurement and conversion of measurements. 4.G.A Draw and identify lines and angles, and classify shapes by properties of their lines and angles.
Grade 5	5.OA.A Write and interpret numerical expressions. 5.NBT.A Understand the place value system. 5.NBT.B Perform operations with multi-digit whole numbers and with decimals to hundredths. 5.NF.B Apply and extend previous understandings of multiplication and division.

Key:
OA = Operations & Algebraic Thinking; NBT = Number & Operations in Base Ten; NF = Number & Operations--Fractions; MD = Measurement & Data; G = Geometry